Sustainable
Democracy

Sept. 21, 1996

George & Harriet,

Thanks for your encouragement
and support on this project.
My conversations with both of you
over the years have been a
stimulus and challenge for this work

Jon Brell

Sustainable Democracy

Individuality and the Politics of the Environment

John Buell & Tom DeLuca

SAGE Publications
International Educational and Professional Publisher
Thousand Oaks   London   New Delhi

For information address:

SAGE Publications, Inc.
2455 Teller Road
Thousand Oaks, California 91320
E-mail: order@sagepub.com

SAGE Publications Ltd.
6 Bonhill Street
London EC2A 4PU
United Kingdom

SAGE Publications India Pvt. Ltd.
M-32 Market
Greater Kailash I
New Delhi 110 048 India

Printed in the United States of America

Library of Congress Cataloging-in-Publication Data

Buell, John.
    Sustainable democracy: Individuality and the politics of the environment / John Buell, Tom DeLuca
       p.   cm.
    Includes bibliographical references (p. 146) and index.
    ISBN 0-7619-0221-X (cloth : acid-free paper). — ISBN 0-7619-0222-8 (pbk. : acid-free paper)
    1. Sustainable development—United States. 2. Democracy—United States. I. DeLuca, Tom, 1946– . II. Title.
HC110.E5B824   1996
338.973—dc20   96-9976

This book is printed with soy ink on recycled paper.

96 97 98 99 10 9 8 7 6 5 4 3 2 1

Production Editor: Michèle Lingre
Designer/Typesetter: Christina Hill
Cover Designer: Michelle Lee

To the memory of our grandparents

*—Salvatore and Margherita DeLuca, Jean and Al Sasso,
Oscar Webber and May Buell—*

And the future of all their great-grandchildren

Contents

Introduction

April 30, 1995, was the 25th anniversary of Earth Day. Like other holidays, this day proved to be an occasion for reflection on accomplishments and failures. Unlike the first Earth Day, however, most Americans now claim they are environmentalists. Corporate executives, union heads, political leaders, grassroots activists, and consumers all pledge their allegiance to "green" values. A poll taken in mid-February of that year—trumpeted on the cover of *Time* magazine—revealed that most Americans now consider environmental values "important" (Thompson, 1995, p. 58). Many even believe them to be "very important."

Oddly enough, the new environmental consciousness grew in an era in which a new conservatism began to dominate the American economic and political landscape. Under Ronald Reagan's leadership, the Republican party made impressive gains at both federal and state levels during the 1980s, setting the stage for the capture of both Houses of Congress in 1994. By the mid-1990s, the self-confidence of conservatives soared to a 70-year high. The political goal became increasingly bold: Not just to modulate the New Deal as Richard Nixon's middle-class Republicanism had tried to do but to discredit and dismantle it. Republicans sought to return to a world governed by the 1920s belief that in seeking profitability, unfettered corporate power also serves the public interest.

Deregulation became the watchword of workplaces, of financial institutions, of transportation. Even with regard to the environment, political leaders endeavored to extend the principles of the market and privatization as far as possible. Debate seemed to extend only to how far and how fast this process should go. The theme of freeing the engines of economic growth from the brakes of government regulation increasingly came to define the mission of both political parties. Indeed, even before Reagan, Democratic President Jimmy Carter had placed deregulation squarely on the White House agenda. Drawing lessons from conservative electoral triumphs, many of today's liberals also want to "reinvent" government.

Conservatives had pressed the issue for years in its starkest terms. If in 1991 they could proudly claim they had shaken the Vietnam syndrome with the invasion of Iraq, by 1995 they could point to the success of a 15-year assault on the Three Mile Island syndrome—the purported urge to impose new health and environmental regulations on corporate investment and technology choices. Seen over time, the change even within dominant Republican thinking was palpable. Whereas Richard Nixon had established the Environmental Protection Agency, Ronald Reagan's goal was to abolish it.

The job of restoring the modern Prometheus to its roaring twenties status has not proven easy, however. Even during Reagan's heyday, calls for environmental regulation continuously arose, phoenix-like, from the ashes. Even in the 104th Congress, the most conservative since the 1920s, environmental protection has to be handled almost as gingerly as the popular Social Security program.

Regular citizens also have been mounting environmental challenges. Despite elaborate efforts to portray itself as the clean fuel of the future, the nuclear industry has not been able to win public acceptance for new facilities. From the perspective of other large corporations, the greatest contemporary problem may be the inability to situate new plants and disposal facilities, a corporate freedom once taken for granted. Opposition to such ventures has become so widespread as to elicit an abbreviation of its own, NIMBY (not in my back yard). Although corporate America understands grassroots protest as simply rearguard and parochial, it does recognize these groups as forces with which it must deal.

In many other places, the so-called 3R campaigns for waste reduction, reuse, and recycling have substantial popular appeal. In addition, however much corporations may fight environmental regulation, they acknowledge the popularity of environmental goals with a host of products labeled "green."

Environmentalism has grown against the odds in the last quarter century. In spite of a conservative political tide and the demands of the freer global market, the environment is a contentious issue in American politics. Environmentalists of all kinds are thorns in the side of corporate conservatives in a way that labor, liberals, and the fragmented left have not recently been able to become.

For their part, many environmental activists remain convinced that, despite some clear gains, the United States has made little progress in such vital areas as the hole in the ozone layer or the greenhouse effect. The most radical environmental groups are even more strident in proclaiming that anthropocentric environmental goals have occasioned few sacrifices by the human community on behalf of nature.

Curiously, many business leaders also seem to believe that economic growth and environmentalism are opponents in a zero-sum game. They are fond of telling us that there is no free lunch and that there will be no lunch at all if onerous and unnecessary environmental regulations are not eased. Meanwhile, mainstream environmental organizations, such as the National Wildlife Federation, the Audubon Society, and the Environmental Defense Fund, and ecologically sensitive business and political leaders fall in between. In their view, corporate interests still place insufficient economic value on environmental assets, but sensible public programs have fostered real progress on several environmental fronts.

The public's reaction reflects the terms of the debate. The *Time* poll (Thompson, 1995) also reveals that people feel both that the nation has not done enough to protect the environment and that environmental regulation hurts the economy. A majority seems willing to make the sacrifice: They too believe there is no free lunch. One striking aspect of the contemporary debate is that each wing shares with the others certain utilitarian assumptions, transmuted and applied to the environment. Any reduction in the number of goods and services produced subtracts, it is assumed, from the net sum of human satisfaction. Humans, left to their own devices, always want more. Believing the threat to nature is from a human nature unartfully defined for the problems we face at this point in history, some radicals want us to suppress—some would censure—human desire. We could move toward "biocentric" values by giving moral primacy to nonhuman nature.

Corporate conservatives, less worried by ecological threats to human health, let alone to nature, believe the real danger from infinite desires lies in not attempting to satisfy them. Such a defeatist course would undermine the engine of self-interest that pulls the train of economic growth, which these conservatives equate with progress itself. Unregulated growth—more goods—is the anthropocentric cure to the disease incident to a human nature that is fulfilled only when allowed to seek to acquire infinitely.

The environmentally conscious public's perception of these issues reflects its popularization in the media. This popularization draws metaphorically on the concern over the national debt regularly articulated by mainstream conservatives and neoliberals. These people suggest that individual profligacy has gotten us into this hole and only individual sacrifice can get us out. When applied to the environment, this theory calls to mind both a hopeful reading of Malthus and a position taken by some radical environmentalists. The accumulated debt to nature generated by years of neglect—including outright use of nature as a sink—has led to an endpoint. We must each pay our share by making sacrifices in the way we live or suffer the consequences.

The sacrifices entailed seem so onerous, however, that we rebel against making them even as we are continually called back to them by the severity of our problems. This logic suggests that such a process will continue until we really bite the bullet or until major environmental catastrophe overwhelms the whole civilization. Society cannot live with environmental regulations and it cannot live without them.

We believe this line of thought is more useful as an illustration of the narrow ideological and theoretical binds in which we are caught than in generating an acceptable response to our social and environmental problems. The task of this book is to weaken the hold of these binds by suggesting the ways in which such arguments are themselves part of our problem. The environmental crisis is real. It is not merely a matter of perceptions. It is, however, also to be understood as a symptom of the inability of contemporary discourse, both corporate and environmentalist, to come to terms with the vagaries and unpredictability of human and nonhuman nature.

We make our case by asking questions about the nature of the debate, about the tacitly shared assumptions of the participants, about the scope of their disagreements. We ask who does and who should benefit from the answers to such questions. Finally, we ask what it means to "resolve" this or any other debate in ethics or public policy.

We ask why, for instance, if environmental debt reduction is so imperative, so many have been unwilling to make the sacrifice. Just who is being asked to do so? How did this particular "we" come to be a particular people with a clearly defined identity? If environmental protection is like a cosmological Federal Reserve Bank, whose job is to "take the punch away just as the party is getting good," can we be so sure the party was as good as advertised? Was everyone invited?

One way into these issues is to recognize that even in an age drenched in social science, the terms of the debate are bound indissolubly to good stories, stories that anchor them, that give them weight, that capture our fancy and drive our fears even more than our intellect. Good stories are more than mythological fantasy. They retain power because they serve as sharp lenses through which we understand our lives, develop our hopes and fears, and locate our places as individuals and as a people.

Good stories, however, are themselves rooted in powerful beginnings that continuously define the kind of story to be told. All the stories we recount can be read as starting with tacit assumptions about a primal origin. We once lived in a "garden of Eden," and then later in a "state of nature." Modern problems result from our exodus, the one forced, the other chosen. Nevertheless these premises, first of the Old Testament and then of philosophical liberalism, have themselves been rewritten into diverging tales of beginnings. The latter is a Promethean tale; the former is a story of Arcadian delights. We call these *myths of origin.*

We begin this story about the complicated politics of the environment with a myth of technological growth. We believe that a careful examination of this myth helps clarify who we think we are as a people and some of the tensions and problems implicit in that identity. We then turn to its opposite, another myth of industrial development, one implicit in the most powerful criticisms of modern industry and technology. This one tells us a lot about why the Promethean myth is never fully satisfying. This second myth is one of lost Edens, a basis for nostalgia and the fantasies allowing us to survive in a Promethean world. We call this Arcadian fantasy *Paradise Lost.*

Despite apparent and real differences, these myths share assumptions on a range of registers. Indeed, in an important sense, they need one another. Environmental and political reconstruction, therefore, requires coming to grips with their similarities as much as their differences.

To begin with, they share deep foundational assumptions of Judeo-Christian society, as well as of philosophical liberalism. People were ordered out of Eden into a "state of nature," to use Thomas Hobbes's phrase (discussed in Kuehls, 1996). They then had to escape from that unholy war of "all against all" into civil society to regulate "private" affairs that too easily could reprise that war. Civil society, however, could not sufficiently temper the evils unleashed by the fall into the state of nature, so a political state became necessary.

Ironically, corporate conservatives embrace liberalism's more optimistic mentor, John Locke. In Locke's view humans created a minimal "public" state to erect legal codes of behavior that would make civil and economic intercourse more smooth and predictable. As outlined in Locke, the danger for corporate conservatives then becomes precisely that state, which must be kept from its natural tendency to interfere with the very liberty its creation was designed to assure.

Equally ironic, many radicals unwittingly embrace liberalism's founder, and premier pessimist, Hobbes. In Hobbes's vision (Kuehls, 1996), individuals give up their sovereignty to a domineering political authority—a Leviathan—to avoid the war of all against all. Modern Hobbesians see this war as one that has been sublimated into a war against nature that destroys both nature and humanity. To end this war against nature, the state must impose as harsh limits on material acquisitiveness as it once imposed on partisan strife.

Some radicals do talk about "returning" to nature—indeed, this fantasy is one indication of their liberalism—but the road on their map actually is a prenatural one whose real destination is Eden. In this Eden, they are the new creators. They seek to mold both nature and human nature according to ecological principles derivable either from science or from listening carefully to nature's rhythms in a way somehow unmediated by the human mind. Some are willing to employ a national regulatory Leviathan that relies on law, courts, and police power to achieve their ends. Many others overtly crave societies in which "small is beautiful." Nonetheless, their call for harmonious natural communities sometimes has the feel of a million mini-Leviathans that depend on severe moral codes and social intrusions into private lives.

Conservatives also take important detours, especially from Locke's (discussed in Kuehls, 1996) view of how property is politically, economically, and morally necessary for human security and independence. They forget how property— broadly conceived, at times, by Locke— also refers to the development of one's capacities. Their view of property, instead, is untroubled by the facts of contemporary American life. Today, the great majority of the public work for others. In addition, conservatives forget that the boards on which they serve are themselves Leviathans that should signal warnings to the true guardians of individual liberty. Look for dangers from other directions.

These opponents in the environmental debate share another set of assumptions. Their beliefs about democracy and the political process itself make it difficult to explore the limits of their myths and related assumptions about human nature, politics, and society. Although ecofundamentalists—those propelled by the myth of Eden—are generally more democratic in their views, both sides implicitly see democracy itself as only incidental to, or perhaps even a barrier to, a sounder society. Indeed, across the environmental spectrum, achieving a sustainable economy is too often seen primarily as a technical problem. For free market environmentalists—those sympathetic both to the environment and to the corporate world—one needs to factor in more fully the cost of nonrenewable resources and hazardous by-products of an otherwise necessary technology. Once this technical chore is accomplished, the market economy can sail along smoothly to maximum growth and environmental security.

Ecofundamentalist solutions are more elusive to understand as technical. Nonetheless, in one version they rely on ecological principles and science. In another, they rely on discoverable principles of spirituality. In neither do they look primarily to democratic politics. Indeed, some radicals believe we have already done such irreversible damage to the planet that we must impose substantial reductions in our access to material goods. Some doubt the willingness of society to accede to such demands. They worry that scarcities and environmental damage will lead to disorganization, war, and the rise of dictatorship. They then may be forced into making a Hobbesian choice: a benevolent, ecologically attentive aristocracy (Ophuls, 1977, p. 227) or a severe authoritarian regime that engages in unjust triage to avoid thorough ecosuicide.

We believe that some of these nightmares could unfold. More than simply premature, however, the retreat in each case is occasioned by a reading of all forms of current growth as "natural" and a failure to open broader democratic discussion of ways to reorient growth and better distribute its rewards. Misapprehensions of this sort make more likely the outcome the retreat is designed to avoid.

We also share the concern that environmental problems do not stand alone. They are threads in a web of social relations that include injustices deserving of remedy—both in the North and in the South and in the relations between them. Indeed, these injustices require remedy if we are to solve environmental problems.

Realistic scenarios do exist that can free us from the nightmare of eco-suicide. But besides political will, they require a reexamination of assumptions, especially about the relation of economic growth to the quality of life, about the social constitution of ideas of growth themselves, and about democracy. In the chapters that follow, we hope to contribute to that reexamination.

In Chapter 1, we begin our analysis by presenting the prototypical myths of origin that undergird so much environmental debate today. We examine why they have such power over us and how we may understand them as partial truths that both illuminate and obscure the task before us. Our starting point is the question of how much opponents in the environmental debate tacitly share. We delve into the possible social consequences of a failure to probe these central assumptions.

In Chapters 2 and 3, we look in detail at the major divergent understandings of sustainable economics. Chapter 2 looks at contemporary corporate environmentalism and its debt to Promethean myths. Underwritten by faith in technology and markets, this myth and its view of nature have shaped corporate responses to—indeed, definitions of—environmental problems. Despite the prevalence of technological optimism in America, however, and the purchase this myth has in centers of power, it continues to generate waves of opposition.

This opposition has taken the form of both grassroots reactions to specific industrial technologies and independent scholars and foundations interested in the development of whole new technologies. We discuss several of these in Chapter 3. They have embraced the proactive task of better wedding ecology, economics, and technology. Throughout the text we also draw out the themes of opposition, as articulated by its more radical members, in order to reveal the major countermyth of Paradise Lost. Although the Promethean is by far the more dominant of these myths, the ecofundamentalist myth plays a major role in shaping the kinds of opposition to technology that surface.

Moreover, this myth sheds important light on the problems of a society organized economically and psychologically around the idea of material growth. At the very least, it poses the question of whether sheer material growth provides the benefits and satisfactions claimed for it. Nonetheless, it has limits of its own. Consideration of these limits provides an important entree into current political controversies. Serving as a major contrast to the dominant myth, its inadequate definition of alternatives sometimes builds political support for its Promethean opponent.

In Chapter 4, we probe another assumption, that these worldviews constitute a simple binary opposition. We suggest instead that they have an intricate relation to one another. Assumptions both opponents paradoxically share regarding democracy, technique, and other fundamental issues may render each inadequate as a guide to reshaping America's political economy in environmentally sound ways. These reflections lead us to ask whether one might make different assumptions about nature, community, and democracy than those shared by all major participants in this controversy. We discuss these contrasting assumptions and the difficult issue of their grounding.

In Chapters 5 and 6, we propose a related set of principles and specific reforms of both the social infrastructure and the modes of work, travel, and leisure. We believe these will enable citizens to lead freer lives of higher quality. Growth along current lines is neither socially nor ecologically sustainable. Unlike ecofundamentalists, however, we question whether the small community of pastoral mythology is any more "natural" than the growth economy, in what sense we should say nature is a "home" for us, and the implications of these beliefs. In addition, we question both the plausibility and the desirability of a no-growth, or negative growth, economy in the contemporary world.

A tempered idea of growth needs to be wedded to broader notions of the quality of life. We believe that such reforms, if embraced in a serious political agenda, will help citizens discover a plausible way out of the bind we now face regarding the simultaneous need for economic growth and environmental security.

Social movements or sets of ideas cannot avoid making assumptions about human purposes. Although we believe that the conception of human goals and aspirations we lay out throughout this book is an appropriate response to the environmental and political problems we face, we do not claim they can be grounded in any ultimate or final sense. We concede our reading to be just that—a reading. In the last chapter, we discuss the nature of these problems of analysis and political dangers implicit in any political agenda and suggest an appropriate stance toward these risks. Nevertheless, we conclude that the goals of democracy and quality of life are essential to environmental sustainability.

Far from being simply deconstructive, our approach suggests a more sustainable form of politics that allows humans to advance compelling goals while resisting the inordinate impositions that even the most noble enterprises often entail. These concerns point us back to another central public issue of our day: democracy itself. Only democratic politics can help us develop real alternatives to the environmentally destructive aspects of our political economy while limiting the impositions and exclusions such a positive agenda inevitably fosters. Our own historic democratic commitment, one of the most attractive characteristics of American society, provides the best basis for an environmentally sustainable future that is also free. Without a broader exploration of how we might defend and enliven it in this new context, democracy may become the planet's most endangered species. That would be an extinction we should all mourn.

Acknowledgments

If most scholarly projects are inevitably collaborative, jointly authored ones are all the more so. This project began with a set of conversations years ago between the authors on the relation of the individual to the community. When we picked up that conversation two years ago, we found that our interest had evolved into a consideration of how the role of the individual in a democratic polity in the late 20th century could foster a high quality of life and a sustainable relationship with the "natural" world. How could we create sustainability without sacrificing individuality, freedom, or democracy?

All chapters of this book involved extensive consultation—including enormous phone bills between Southwest Harbor, Maine and New York City—and thoroughly joint writing by both authors. While Chapters 1, 2, 3, 6, and 7 were entirely collaborative, Buell did slightly more initial work on Chapters 4 and DeLuca on Chapter 5.

In the process of our writing and research, we were fortunate in being able to draw on a number of our colleagues. Biologist John Anderson first alerted us to controversies within scientific ecology bearing on our thesis. Ongoing discussions on the history and practice of environmental politics with Alesia Maltz and John Visvader helped us sharpen our themes. Michael Kraft and Joel Kassiola gave helpful advice on our manuscript, as did other colleagues at conferences at which we presented early drafts of chapters of this book. The work of Barry Commoner has been both instructive and inspirational.

Fordham University political science faculty have helped in many ways. By encouraging DeLuca to develop a course on environmental politics and law, they allowed him to further pursue his longstanding interest in this area. He is particularly grateful to his colleagues on the Lincoln Center campus,

Nicole Fermon, Susan Berger, Ralph Meyer, and Susan Beck for their strong support. The Rose Hill campus faculty were especially gracious, warmly welcoming him into the newly united bi-campus political science department. He wishes, therefore, also to thank Bruce Andrews, William Baumgarth, Bruce Berg, John Entelis, Martin Fregus, Richard Fleisher, Dale Nelson, Mary Nichols, Rev. Richard Regan SJ, Christianna Hardy—and especially Paul Kantor and David Lawrence whose interest in and supportive comments on his prior work, *The Two Faces of Political Apathy*, helped build confidence for this one. He also gratefully acknowledges the generous support of Dean Ed Bristow, and all those on the Lincoln Center Fordham staff, especially Lois Cucurullo and Candy Sturm.

Students of both authors have helped in many ways. DeLuca wishes especially to thank those in his environmental politics and law classes. Each helped him see that our vision today should also engender a serious—but realistic—program for an environmentally sustainable future. It should not dwell on a lost past—real or imagined—that never can be reclaimed. We hope this book is of some help in preparing them well for that task.

Buell would especially like to thank David Malakoff who provided important insights into the politics of contemporary environmental organizations. A series of discussions he had with Jennifer Judd on feminism and civil liberties helped us frame key issues. Andrea Perry and Debra Lucey helped with research and aided us in the preparation of the index. In addition to intellectual stimulation, all four were personally supportive during those inevitable down times that accompany any such undertaking.

Outside our own immediate colleagues, we both owe a substantial debt to other scholars. For one of us, an undergraduate course with George Kateb on American political theory helped spur lifelong interest in the field. For the other, a kindness shown by David Abbott encouraged him to think he had the ability to do something useful in the world of political thinking. Later, from graduate school days on, William Connolly's support, brilliance, and inspiration have helped guide both of us.

Jane Bennett's work on Thoreau helped us clarify our central themes. Her meticulous criticisms of two earlier versions of the work were invaluable. Tom Dumm helped us connect our themes more closely to issues in international politics and provided extensive bibliographical suggestions. Peter Bachrach read an early draft and talked extensively with both of us about the politics of class, race, and gender. Discussions with Jean Elshtain on community and the politics of the body helped us clarify some of the themes in Chapter 4. Juliet Schor shared with us early drafts of her studies on overwork, the decline of leisure time, and consumerism.

We also wish to extend special thanks to Carrie Mullen, who was social science acquisition editor at Sage Publications when this project commenced. Carrie discussed the project at length with both of us, encouraged us in its pursuit, and ensured that the publication process was on track before she departed. Renée Piernot then provided prompt and careful assistance in its completion.

Finally, no project of this sort can be completed without help on the home front. Susan Covino Buell commented constructively on many of the themes in this work. Todd Buell's fundamentalist critique of them helped give new meaning to the idea of intergenerational conflict, but always within the confines of good humor and respect. Elisabeth and Timothy Buell were supportive throughout their father's long absences "in the computer room" or on the telephone—again?!"

DeLuca wishes to thank his parents, Thomas and Katherine DeLuca, and his brother Robert for *always* being there. He also is grateful to friends who have been especially supportive this year—Norma, Alan, Cookie, Kathy, Robin, Maria, Mike, Jack, Aaron, and Annika. He also thanks Judith at the Cornelia Street Cafe for her good humor, his friends at Bleecker Street Pastry, especially Carmem and Mônica for their kindness and wisdom, and Joe for his good, strong, black coffee, and his buddies on his softball teams, the *Bandits* and the *Kettle of Fish*, especially Patrick and Adriane.

The canons of authorship of course require that we acknowledge omissions and problems as our responsibility. We do so willingly. We hope, however, our readers —both friends and critics— take these up as a challenge to solve the serious problems that face us all.

1 Myths of Origin

Two Modern Fantasies

Modern Americans live with a dilemma. We take pride in the ways our national wealth has allowed us to become a society of consumers, whereas we quietly worry that our modes of consumption are a threat to our environment and even to our health. Consumption, the solution to one set of problems, has become the cause of another. Nonetheless, more consumption often seems the only practical solution to the problems created by the industrial and postindustrial economic engines that make consumption itself possible. Is this a dilemma we must simply live with? To answer this question, we need to examine more closely our own assumptions about human and nonhuman nature, about technology and society, and ultimately about our relation to the environment. In addition, we need to explore not just the attitudes that propel consumption but also those that demonize it.

To explore these attitudes and assumptions, we must probe those myths of origin that are their source and provide continuing spiritual sustenance for them. In the United States, there is no better place to explore mythology than in the world of popular consumerism, no better time to do so than the Christmas season, and no commodity more interesting for this purpose than the automobile. As it has been from the beginning, the automobile is a screen on which some of Americans' deepest fears, hopes, and aspirations are projected and a repository in which they are collected.

Consider two television advertising backdrops against which to observe the American car. The first consists of a deserted rural road, perched hundreds of feet above a beautiful body of water, guarded by finely sculpted stone. The sky is blue, so blue the few white clouds call attention not to themselves but to the sky's perfection. To complete this backdrop, a conventionally attractive young woman is speeding happily along. Now the foreground. She is in a Lincoln Continental.

In the second, a male in his late 20s or early 30s lies on a couch suspended in space on one side of the television screen. On the other side, we see a space station and watch the couch and man drift closer to it as we listen to Aaron Copeland's *Appalachian Spring*. What is in the space station? An Oldsmobile.

Although many readings are possible, the themes most evident in these commercials are clearly and relentlessly played out in American advertising. Cars are a way to escape the tedium, pressure, and ugliness of urban life to a quiet and spectacular communion with an unspoiled nature or with a nature in space, beyond human contamination. Consider how many vehicles today are pictured as virtual spaceships, providing self-contained worlds and sources of power allowing the driver unparalleled control. Consider how many times one sees cars in television ads in rural settings, whether beside horse farms or moving through small villages.

The people in such ads reflect the ethnic and racial diversity of our people more accurately than in the past. Nonetheless, there is a middle-class solidity about them, in their confident demeanor, their possession of valued skills, their smart dress, and their comfortable homes. They are healthy, happy, and often in love. Most important, they are a middle class no longer burdened with society's or nature's problems. Whether in space or in the country, the modern car has enabled them to transcend all physical limitations and social dangers and distresses. They are free.

The view of the world as seen in these advertisements has parallels in other venues of our popular culture.[1] Theme parks provide two ostensibly different paths away from daily worries. On one hand, one can find futuristic celebrations of technology in such complexes as Disney's Epcot center. On the other hand, these parks feature retrospective views of a world left behind. Both notions replicate idealizations popular with audiences at world fairs throughout this century.

Andrew Ross (1994) describes in detail the Polynesian Cultural Center in Hawaii. Visitors to the center are treated to picturesque recreations of a primitive people living a life of simple harmonies, grounded in a handicraft economy, with social relations of mutuality, and existing in a nonexploitative relationship to the land. Ross is compelling in calling such pictures into question. He is even more persuasive in suggesting that these displays appeal "to genuine popular anxiety about the future of human settlements in our technologically saturated world" (p. 53).

The realm of popular social theory as portrayed in American political magazines shows the same dualism. Commendations of technology's promises are often pitted against a popular literature that celebrates what we have lost in terms of social or natural simplicity. In this intellectual world, however, the balance seems more heavily weighted toward the celebration of technology.

In the face of regulation, some of the leading defenders of corporate growth have done far more than simply lobby against particular forms of legislation. Rather than directly address environmental concerns, they choose instead to remind Americans of what they regard as our industrial heritage and the ways that heritage makes us the kind of people we are.

Prometheus Unbound

Writing after the *Challenger* disaster, Henry Fairlie, a senior editor of *The New Republic,* ridicules what he regards as a pervasive fear of technological innovation among the U.S. populace. Drawing on the work of anthropologist Mary Douglas, he argues that definitions of risks are culturally constructed. He suggests that the growing American fear of death from modern technology processes and its products is an outgrowth of a burgeoning obsession with individual rights. An unreasonable and culturally specific definition of risk, therefore, is standing in the way of widespread social progress.

To make his point, Fairlie (1986) compares reactions in his day to those 19 years before, following a deadly capsule fire in the early stages of the *Apollo* program. Citizens of that earlier era mourned, but then redoubled their efforts to surmount difficulties. In the intervening years, a sense of fear and risk had overcome them:

the idea that our individual lives and the nation's life can and should be risk free has grown into an obsession, driven far and deep into American attitudes. Indeed, the idea of a risk free society is one of the most debilitating influences in American life today, progressively enfeebling the economy with a mass of safety regulations and a widespread fear of liability rulings, and threatening to create an uninventive and unbuoyant society. . . . This is a strikingly American phenomenon, one that seems to have taken root in yet another distortion of the philosophy of rights underlying the Constitution, as if the Declaration of Independence had been rewritten to include freedom from risk among the self-evident rights to life, liberty, and the pursuit of happiness. . . . If America's new timorousness had prevailed among the Vikings, their ships and their bold prows but frail hulls would have been declared unseaworthy. The Norsemen would have stayed home and jogged. (pp. 14-16)

Fairlie (1986) argues that this distortion in the original meaning of the founding documents is explicable as an outgrowth of the increasing role that bureaucrats, planners, and professionals have come to exercise in American life. Because people in these lines of work do not make or do things, they have little regard and respect for, or understanding of, the value of these activities.

Fairlie's argument is worthy of close analysis. The heady optimism about technology to which it speaks, with its emphasis on new worlds discovered and the purpose given to life by such discoveries, is evocative of central elements of our culture. This fact alone, however, should give us pause. Fairlie tells us, for example, that the Norse were people of purpose and courage who single-handedly embarked on dangerous voyages, the consequence of which was geographical and intellectual new worlds.

We could begin our analysis by turning Fairlie's cultural relativism back on him. We might ask whether the Norse were engaged in the modern risk-taking adventure Fairlie calls "discovery" or in ancient religious or geographical purposes of their own, however opaque these may be to us.

There is an even more important question: Why, if such adventurous missions of discovery and innovation foster deeply ennobling and self-confirming ends, would there ever be a desire to put a limit on them?

To answer, let us follow the image of economic development that Fairlie presents and see if it creates problems for his account of recent political developments. Fairlie correctly assumes that modern industrial society was partly constituted by a new orientation to the natural and human worlds. Medieval and premodern conceptions of the world had conceived it as an expression of an underlying order of meaning, culminating in God. The human task was to understand that order through the word of God and to take one's place in it. Such a view was inscribed in social and political practices, from the ways in which property was inherited to how monarchs were made hereditary, how laws were based on precedent, how marriages were arranged between parties of like station, and so on. It was not the case that such societies were never technologically innovative. Rather, technology was seen as society's handmaiden, simply one expression of the social order, and its role was limited accordingly. For such societies, death itself was not only an organic part of the natural order of existence but the medium through which nature and temporality were transcended.[2]

That medieval conception broke down. Part of the theological aspects of the breakdown lay in subtle tensions within a worldview that was not as simple and uniform as its defenders imagined. A sovereign God was seen as standing atop, or as the culmination of, an invariant order. But wherein lies the sovereignty of God if the order He stands atop is seen as unchangeable? Out of these confusions and tensions emerged a new worldview, though one that was indebted to its religious origins. It suggested that the power and transcendence of God were profaned by declaring any part of the social or natural world as sacred or as an expression of the sacred. Human beings could and must establish a nonidolatrous relation to the world through their demonstrated ability to understand and control that world. Their success in achieving such control was a sign that they had achieved a proper relation to God and the world, and their material success in that world was a manifestation of God's favor.

Laissez-faire economics fit this emerging religious worldview well, but extended it in significant ways. From the beginning, laissez-faire economics was wedded to a conception of scientific rationalism, through which the world could be understood in a causal sense and such knowledge and control could be promoted. The establishment of minimal housing and comfort were seen as means to longer life. In addition, the extension of life was viewed not merely as an end in itself but as proof that one had gained even further knowledge and control over the natural world. It is arguable in terms consistent with Fairlie's (1986) reasoning that once the market is able to achieve a degree of food, shelter, and clothing for a large segment of the population, consumers will turn to questions of premature death, indeed, to the idea of unnecessary death itself and—in the most extreme form—why people die.

In the late 1960s—the period Fairlie points to as the origin of our malady—it became evident to many that the system had failed to recognize that certain classes of persons had been excluded from enjoying the benefit of a long life. Efforts grew to assess health and mortality prospects, to correlate these with occupational and community sites, and to try to construct a set of causal regularities based on this work, to develop what some call a *popular epidemiology.* Such conclusions were and are subject to methodological criticisms. What is less well attended, however, is the way they are consistent with the evolution of the worldview Fairlie believes is being undermined. In taking aim at a counterproductive obsession with risks, Fairlie fails to consider how this obsession is implicit in even the earliest development of market philosophy and the reformed Protestantism that accompanied it. These philosophies promised knowledge and control of nature and the prospect that well-being and health could be extended throughout the population.

One may apply a similar discussion to Fairlie's (1986) ideas about rights. He protests the willingness of citizens to claim that their rights are violated by the deployment of certain technologies. This doctrine of individual rights—especially the right to appeal to the courts to be compensated for damage to one's body and property—stands in the way of social progress. Nonetheless, in overtly attacking one sort of rights, Fairlie obsessively but tacitly defends another, that of the right to deploy technologies as the managers of large-scale enterprises see fit.[3] Furthermore, he seeks the public's blessing, sanctioned in property rights law.

Fairlie does not explain or say anything about the origins of just how and why one right should take precedence over another. Fairlie's concern with property rights is less simple in application than he assumes. For one of the factors leading to the "obsession" with risk aversion was the perception that industrial facilities were seen as making one's home—a longstanding form of private property—less safe and secure. The ideals of economic expansion, scientific rationalism, and rights themselves on which Fairlie premises his attack, are not as simple or uniform in their application to an evolving order as Fairlie suggests.

Fairlie attempts to protect his analysis against the suspicion that his ideals themselves may point in directions different from those he specifies. His discussion of how the bureaucratic mentality is given the room to do its misdeeds is tacit acknowledgment that other implications remain unaccounted for. By his own analysis, the public goes along with the fears generated about industrial progress because it has lost "faith" in the direction of industrial civilization itself.

Indeed, the public has lost some faith in the unitary understanding of U.S. market and scientific traditions Fairlie suggests to be definitive. Once probed more deeply, however, this loss of faith may represent public doubt in Fairlie's unvarnished reading of these ideals and a different, perhaps more comprehensive, application of them to contemporary life's problems. This suggests that readings other than Fairlie's are plausible. For example, increased public confidence in the science of ecology is one instance of scientific rationalism moving in a path different from the one Fairlie endorses. Modern ecology constitutes both a loss of faith in his reading of progress and increased faith in a more nuanced alternative.

Both are derivatives of scientific rationalism, however. Indeed, for Fairlie (1986) to worry about a loss of faith at all may indicate that—because some accounts he opposes have important ties to his own—he can ill afford to acknowledge these perspectives as serious alternatives. To do so would be to resurrect a set of reasonable political questions of late modernity, questions not reducible to unreflective measurements of progress consistent only with his view. These include to what purposes progress should be put? This entails the subquestion: How much should avoidance of risks to health or other forms of danger be a goal of modern life? By trying to retrieve faith for one historical application of market and scientific ideals, Fairlie's analysis obscures others. The implications of his use of faith in this selective way for the whole structure of his argument are never considered.

Similar arguments and strategies are implicit in another of the popular defenders of industrial progress. Julian Simon, a professor of economics and business administration at the University of Maryland, is famous for a bet made with biologist Paul Ehrlich on the future price of resources. Simon (1985) repudiates Ehrlich's notion that we are "running out of everything." Simon won the bet, but of more importance for our purposes is his line of reasoning. Simon suggests that economic and population growth are the answer to any problems they create. They achieve this result through three mechanisms: price, human initiative, and ultimate expansion of markets.

Simon's theory is based on a repudiation of Malthus, and especially those Simon calls doomsayers, who apply Malthusian thinking to long-run resource and environmental problems. Simon charges these doomsayers with errone-ously believing that the world is one of fixed resources and, rigidly following the law of diminishing returns, believing that population growth inexorably drives up resource cost. This thinking, Simon asserts, is applicable only to the short run. In the long run in a free society—by which he means one that respects economic liberty, the rights of property, and markets—the increased price of resources creates an incentive to develop cheaper resources. This goal can be pursued by exploiting present resources more efficiently, by using different available ones, or by discovering new ones. These can then be provided at a comparatively lower price.

The short-run problem therefore creates an economic opportunity to profit that, in the long run, leads inexorably to more and better resources. Historical trends demonstrate, Simon (1985) reports, that the price of resources univer-sally has declined over time. For example, food per capita is growing on a worldwide basis; prices of key raw materials are down; acres of farmland are expanding rather than contracting. Moreover, as population and markets grow, economies of scale evolve along with them, as does the number of citizens whose education and talents allow them to devise new solutions to common problems.

Problems of shortages of key resources (or, we might add, the development of new needs) therefore stimulate new creative activity through the pricing mechanism. Therefore, the short-run problems of resource scarcity created by population and income growth lead directly to the long-run solution of ever more resources. This process, Simon argues, will continue infinitely if not interfered with by unwise social regulation.

Like Fairlie (1986), Simon (1985) acknowledges popular concerns about environmental issues and explains them by blaming doomsayers in the media and government. For Simon, the media is a main culprit: The media can make more money by propagating stories of short-run gloom rather than long-run achievement.

As in Fairlie's (1986) account, Simon's (1985) answer begs a critical question. Why is the public susceptible to these appeals, especially because almost all the media—unlike Fairlie's bureaucrats, planners, and professionals—are market institutions that often respond to consumer demands? Is the media creating the demand out of whole cloth or has a loss of faith by the public rendered it pliant? If it is a loss of faith, is it in progress or even markets as such, or in the ability of markets as currently constituted to protect the public from environmental harm?

Simon's (1985) account is quite revealing. For one thing, he focuses on the market's beneficial effects primarily with regard to one set of problems: long-range resource depletion. He does give other evidence of positive trends. For example, he reports that air and water pollution have decreased during the last several decades. Nevertheless, he neither demonstrates how the pricing mechanism of the market has contributed to this nor does he mention political agitation, government regulation, and consumer demand as causal agencies.

Simon (1985) seems to disdain any government regulation designed to restrain market excesses. Is Simon prepared to argue, first, that pollution is down because of the pricing mechanism, and second, that its beneficial effect is so powerful that it overcame doomsayer meddling?

In fact, the public's skepticism about all-or-nothing attitudes toward the equity available through current markets is perhaps explained when one considers another implication of Simon's (1985) analysis that he does not pursue. Simon reports that, measured by price, the only important resource that is becoming scarce is people. This is demonstrated because the cost of using human mental and physical labor—income—is rising. Although Simon's "facts" on median income are even more difficult to sustain today (c.f. Bowles, Gordon, & Weisskopf, 1993), his analysis of scarcity and price change has implications that he may not wish to acknowledge for one factor of production, human beings.

Consider the implications: People with initiative will see in high labor prices an opportunity to make a profit by increasing the supply of this resource. From a market perspective, their actions will have the long-run effect of driving down price. One way to do this would be to increase the resource called "the productive worker," perhaps by finding ways to get more work out of existing productive workers.[4] Another would be to find a different resource, now called "the highly educated very productive worker," by further automating technology, lessening the utility of the old one. Still another would be to find a new resource called "the robot," making both of the old resources now obsolete.[5]

If Simon's (1985) argument holds, an unrestricted market will always solve the problem of the scarcity of resources by devising ways to find or develop more, different, or new resources. In this case, however, the abundance created is people with lower incomes (the price of the human resource) and lowered standards of living. The wage stagnation of the last 25 years in the United States, for example, could be interpreted as evidence that this is occurring. If it is occurring for the reasons that Simon's model predicts, this may be a reason the public might not fully embrace Simon's absolute faith in the kinds of markets he calls "free." Indeed, the public may suspect that, removed from theory, the actual markets Simon celebrates may have coercive elements not clearly revealed in the formal laissez-faire principles that loan them legitimacy. In addition, the public may believe that material productivity—however important—is still only one goal of civilized living. This purpose is sometimes in tension with other values better represented in religion, tradition, and ethics.

Let's reconsider the Simon-Ehrlich bet to ferret out another important consideration it suggests, but which neither Simon nor Ehrlich pursues. Simon demonstrates that his model, within the terms of current market structures and distributions of power, does have some capacity to predict future resource availability. It clearly also warns us against making long-range doomsday predictions based on simple extrapolations of mathematically identified short-range trends. We should take this point very seriously.

Simon's (1985) argument, however, is not one about inherent unpredictability; indeed, it is quite the contrary. His debate with Ehrlich is about how to predict; both thinkers seem to believe that if one is careful, prediction is not inherently a difficult process. For his part, Simon has great faith in his ability to predict, even in that most difficult of areas, the long run. But this faith, like Fairlie's (1986) belief in technology, is rooted in the same scientific rationalism that has for some time questioned the simple predictive model of "normal science" to which Simon is also indebted. These doubts can be located across the board, from physics, especially the Heisenberg uncertainty principle, to the ecological sciences to the human sciences[6] to the meteorological study of changes in the world's climate.

When one adds the difficulty of predicting the outcome of human-nonhuman intercourse, Simon's (1985) failure to assess the implications of these strands of scientific rationalism for his own thinking is only deepened. To exemplify, we turn to the thorny area of global warming.

Simon claims that virtually all responsible scientific analysts now agree that population and economic growth will not cause resource depletion. Therefore, unfettered markets, expanding to fill the needs created, pose no environmental threat. A consensus based on the same concepts and methodologies Simon uses to legitimize his predictions of future resource availability is building slowly within the scientific community. This perspective suggests that global warming may indeed be occurring, with some of its effect being caused by human overuse of certain resources (French, 1990).

Simon might say that his model can handle even this eventuality because as global warming becomes more apparent, the price of resources that cause it (fossil fuels, herds of ruminants, etc.) will increase. Price increases will create an economic opportunity to find or invent other resources. What in the market will drive up the price of abundant and useful but dangerous resources and create this opportunity? Most likely these price changes will be the result of government regulation or taxation of some kind, perhaps prompted by voter demands.

The very style of social intervention that Simon (1985) excoriates may be required to price the offending resources so high that their use will be dramatically curtailed or ended. Or they could be banned outright. Of course, consumer preferences could change, depressing demand. Nevertheless, in Simon's theory, there is no economic reason—and this is the only one he counts—why, for example, drivers should use gasoline that is relatively cheap more prudently and efficiently than is their current practice. Relevant concerns for health, stability, and survival exist, as do even broader economic reasons and moral considerations about future generations. They are entirely absent from his narrative, however.

These problems are deepened if one is not sure that global warming is occurring and, if it is, to what degree humans are responsible. This awareness may come too late to avoid passing fail-safe threshold points beyond which there is no return—at least not without great suffering. Even if pricing shifts occurred solely through unregulated market mechanisms, an assumption not confidently shared even by free market environmentalists, the shifts would have to happen in time to restore or replace ecological balances. Somehow, the price of the abundant but dangerous resource would have to reflect the danger to the threatened one—and in a timely fashion. We cannot even rely on the price of the limited resource to change market behavior indirectly because it might still be relatively plentiful at the very time other critical environmental thresholds are being passed.

Specifically, present farmland may not become scarce enough to foster market-oriented efforts to save or create substitutes for it until well after we have a clear concept of what global warming—whose full effects we may still be unsure of—will later do to it. Can we really trust land speculators to bet large enough sums on the 50% chance of major crop land loss 30 years from now? How predictable is the patience of capital in our current market economy? Don't forces within markets themselves affect capital's willingness to think long term?

The example of global warming points to an inherent unpredictability, or at least a limited predictability, in the intercourse between humans and the natural world that is thoroughly unaccounted for in Simon's (1985) model. The complexity of nature and human nature may outstrip that of even the best scientific models; the market, especially as Simon construes it, is simply too insensitive to reflect essential complexities of either accurately. Using only Simon's framework, we are left with the hope that global warming will not really occur or, if it does, that markets will somehow appropriately adjust or nature will provide.

Imagine a scenario in which global warming begins to have gradual but severe economic and socially destructive effects (Stevens, 1995). The call very likely would go out for political intervention and would get more strident as the situation becomes more desperate. Belief in the predictability of human intercourse within ecological systems could issue in an authoritarian, if not totalitarian, effort to impose predictability on an environmental crisis that was propagated, in equal measure, by our faith in social and environmental predictability and the unpredictability of each, both singly and in interaction. Extreme political regulation of the market—and the body politic—might then become truly onerous and inevitable. This result is precisely the one Simon (1995) wishes most to avoid but that he begins to invite when he concludes,

> In the short run, all resources are limited. . . . The longer run, however, is a different story. The standard of living has risen along with the size of the world's population since the beginning of recorded time. There is no convincing economic reason why these trends toward a better life should not continue indefinitely. (pp. 305-306)

Simon's (1985, 1995) view of the economic development of the West elides other important political issues as well. Has not much of the capital accumulation, which Simon and Fairlie (1986) rightly, if unreflectively, celebrate, often been itself a product of mercantile and sometimes imperial collaborations between governments and private enterprises? Have these not sometimes constituted effective, if periodic, monopoly domination over markets? How are we to factor into his recipe for a better life the human misery that also goes along with such accumulation, from extermination of populations to slavery to oppressive working conditions to war?

Certainly the history of other historical modes of economics and social life are replete with stories of the human losses entailed, but that does not excuse us from exploring those that populated our own. Are we satisfied with the response that these are simply to be understood as the price of progress, for which there were and are no alternatives? Simon might respond that truly free markets and trade would have avoided these calamities. But that would be to admit that the accumulation built on industrial growth was not accomplished solely through markets free of strong government support.

By restricting his meaning of *economic* to his view of market forces, Simon (1985, 1995) effectively reads outside of economics qualitative dimensions of what a better life could mean. He implies that only free markets, as he defines that term, should determine production. We think he means that, in the end, consumers, workers, and entrepreneurs acting as individuals will and should always be able to decide what things improve their lives. Absent in this reading, however, are the means by which consumers, workers in the market of free labor, and entrepreneurs would be more fully free to assess whether or not production technologies and their consequences meet their real needs. The decision by a few to buy tracts of undeveloped shore land may leave each more happy for a time and no one substantially worse off. Over time, however, as more and more buy the land, everyone's access to the shore is altered and even current owners come to enjoy fewer of the qualities for which they bought the land in the first place.

Nonetheless, in Simon's (1985, 1995) model there is no mechanism for consideration of the possibly deleterious social effects that emerge when large numbers of people engage in practices that are not problematic in small numbers. Market societies, of course, are premised on, justified by, and encourage each of us to get some piece of the action. Simon's attenuated view of the role of politics and his faith in markets as natural and complete may give us too few tools for moving toward a better quality of life.

Finally, Simon also gives little guidance in answering a premier moral question raised by environmental discourse: What are our responsibilities to future generations? The public increasingly questions whether we can continue to use the nonhuman world as a sink even if we could infinitely extract resources from it. Some are just beginning to wonder if we are doing enough to ensure a sufficient worldwide supply of undeveloped land for agriculture should major climactic changes occur. What are the ecological, political, and human consequences of uneven world food and resource distribution? From where comes the faith that sheer economic productivity, without widespread consumer awareness, will not further harm environmental quality? Or that endless geometric population growth will not destroy our most impoverished global neighbors?

Fairlie's (1986) and Simon's (1985, 1995) works are significant because they expose so clearly the contours of faith in industrial progress and the kinds of strategies used to buttress such faith. Close attention to those strategies allows us to make a kind of internal critique of both, one that remains indebted to their ideals. From such a perspective, we can understand why a certain form of economic growth would be both celebrated and resisted. Belief in the need for development of science and technology and the hope for growth are ways to expand knowledge and control over our lives. These narratives, however, also can be read to suggest ways in which we are disadvantaged by technology, acquisitive material growth, and even unreflective "knowledge." Such tensions become especially crucial if nature is not as predictable and manipulable as it often is presumed to be.

Paradise Lost

The possible limits of an unreflective industrial worldview become more apparent from the vantage point of some widely read alternative perspectives. Since the late 1960s, theorists have tried to portray economic growth as a kind of trap or social addiction. Their picture does suggest some reasons why growth might be problematic. Nevertheless, these scenarios remain indebted to myths of origin subject to similar tensions and omissions. First, we attempt a synthetic and highly schematic reconstruction of the kind of general historiography that we believe this myth depends on. We then move specifically to the work of Ivan Illich (1978, 1981) and Karl Polanyi (1957), seminal figures of this discourse. Again our mode is to explicate the model first and then move to an internal critique, focusing especially on internal tensions.

Imagine that we live in a late-19th-century American farming community. We need not assume that the community is literally self-sufficient. It imports some of its tools and a variety of manufactured household goods. Itinerant merchants offer special goods, which some locals prize. Residents still, however, grow most of their own food and build their own homes. There is a village green, with small shops and homes scattered about. Citizens heat their homes with wood and can walk to most of the places they need to reach for day-to-day needs.

This is not a utopian community. There are inequalities; some citizens have managed to be better at crafts and at their retailing. Some farmers are more adept and work harder than others. Even so, land still remains available and most citizens can hope to earn enough to own their own land within a reasonable period of time.

Let us assume further that in the early years of the 20th century, the automobile is marketed to this community. Some wealthy farmers buy the auto. It provides obvious convenience. They can drive to big city stores that they once visited only infrequently and from which they usually purchased goods only through catalogues. Furthermore, autos initially are not associated with any known social problem besides occasional noise and periodic mechanical problems, something well-skilled farmers are equipped to handle.

The auto increases the geographic mobility of its possessors; in this case, they are the ones with the most discretionary income. Stores in a number of surrounding communities now appeal to folks in an expanding radius. Successful merchants offer both more and cheaper products. Eventually, merchants who are less successful find they have to charge more just to survive; some are forced out of business.

Nonetheless, business expansion and economies of scale are producing more communal wealth. Eventually, the car spreads from the wealthy to the upper-middle class, including the successful tradespeople and the moderately successful farmers. They too want the transportation opportunities available to their most successful neighbors, if only to be able to compete for access to goods and services. Their purchase and use of the auto intensifies the phenomena we are discussing. New roads are constructed, making travel to stores at a greater distance more feasible. Disparities grow between small and less successful stores, which appeal mainly to those who can walk or come via horse-drawn carriages, and stores that have been able to establish larger regional clientele and better prices.

In a society where other forms of establishing one's sense of place and purpose are attenuating, commodity consumption takes on more psychic significance. In response, citizens feel an increasing need to own cars, mainly for immediate practical reasons but also for reasons of community status.

As cars become more widely used, other obvious changes occur in social life. Traffic becomes a more common and more widely discussed phenomenon. More of the most successful local merchants move out of the center of the village to surrounding areas that newly constructed roads have made accessible, free of the problems of downtown. Construction of roadways in and out of the village along with the need for parking spaces change the village in important ways. Some trees must be removed to accomodate larger and more numerous roadways and parking lots, and the new paved roads and parking lots reflect more heat than village greens or pathways. Villages become somewhat hotter and less attractive in the summer. The village square is also maintained less well as the tax base erodes with the exodus or closing of important retail businesses. Other technologies abet this process. As refrigerators become items of upper- and middle-class consumption, ice is no longer delivered to homes. Many middle-class citizens must buy refrigerators to store goods that they now can only purchase on a less frequent basis from more distant shops.

Refrigeration technology spawns the growth of air conditioning, which further lessens public commitment to maintenance of parks, trees, and shaded areas. All these purchases deplete income available for taxes, whereas purchasing goods outside the town's taxing jurisdiction further erodes the town's tax base. In any case, some citizens care much less about local amenities now that they can drive out into the countryside and have invested considerable resources in buying the car that makes such trips possible.

The outward push of stores and people requires wider roads; newer roads pushing out even further place a renewed premium on the auto and change the character of the countryside as well. In some cases, private purchase of the most desirable spots eliminates access to traditionally favored views for most citizens.

As markets become larger, the businesses most successful in achieving economies of scale in the new economic environment thrive while smaller ones falter or fail. More and more people find themselves working for others, whereas the increased pace and intensity of competition for jobs make them less secure.

Meanwhile, economic centralization and concentration alter work life as well. The larger partnerships or corporations in which citizens now work are places where workers and managers do not know each other and for whom ownership may take the absentee form. Where owners are absentee and businesses become just one more commodity, it becomes easier to develop a short-term outlook on both one's workers and the future of one's business.

For the large corporate firm, ownership and management are often in separate hands. As a result, profits may no longer be automatically reinvested in the expansion of the business. They go instead as dividends to the relatively wealthy owning class. Oversaving by the rich, along with relatively low wages and underconsumption by the working class, may result in periodic bouts of unemployment. Changes in technology create economic incentives for job redesign, but other motives can also be at work. Increasingly specialized jobs are ones in which craft is no longer necessary and work is repetitive and rote. Both developments weaken incentive to work and lessen workers' bargaining power. In such a workplace, workers often need more supervision to stay on task.

As these changes occur, the society nonetheless becomes more affluent. A growing number and variety of products are produced as well as expected by a widening population of workers and consumers. As the poor and middle class see the obvious gains that the rich have derived, for example from cars and air conditioning, they too hope to achieve these.

Changes also breed poorly understood frustrations, however, and as society evolves, it may increasingly need to rely on fantasy to drive it. The tools of economic growth, the hope for prosperity, and the belief in independence seem to work reasonably well for those in a position to get there first. The culture continually suggests that everyone can get there first. Unfortunately, however, opportunities usually are generated in direct proportion to one's place at the starting gun. Even for the successful, though, the race never seems to end. The chase after the rainbow is engaged, but this adds in imperceptible ways to the uneasiness.

As solid, old-fashioned needs for community, time, and independence become harder to meet, satisfactions are more easily found by sublimating these in commodity purchases. In an anonymous world whose insecurities are multiplied by the structure of opportunity, work, and community, in milieus in which word of mouth is both less common and counts for less, advertising gains greater purchase. And as mobility and immigration become more common, commodities can even more easily be portrayed as a means to social acceptance for newcomers and as the way to maintain status for old timers (Ewen & Ewen, 1992).

Even as many of the most important goods of the emerging industrial economy become widely available, however, they quietly cease to be luxuries. The car is again illustrative. Things spread out. Citizens often do not work where they live and now require cars to get to work or to purchase items that once were available within walking distance. However necessary the car may have become, it takes enormous amounts of time to earn the cash needed for its purchase and maintenance (Gorz, 1980).

The car itself creates other demands that citizens must meet. Maintenance of highways and emergency services require higher taxes, draining potential funds from other purposes. These costs become an obligation of the entire society on the grounds that cars are now basic to life. Cars themselves continually change, in part due to technological innovation, but market strategies also are designed to exploit these innovations. Needing to replace former symbols of status and being less capable of simply repairing the old model because of limited time and declining mechanical literacy, consumers become more willing to accept the changes. Children especially are affected by these changes in status cues. Parents become increasingly concerned about the declining social and economic opportunities available to older children without cars while also fearing for their safety in them.

Consumers soon find themselves buying new cars every few years and needing more than one car at a time. The more necessary the car, the less of a luxury it seems to become. Highway traffic slows the commute and the pace of the shopping outing. Street noise and congestion grow and increased power and speed make auto accidents more likely and more dangerous. The search for the parking space becomes a war of all against all.

What is true of cars becomes true of a wide range of newly available products. No longer luxuries, they become necessities of modern life and in the process paradoxically lose some of their promised value. The modern manufacturer and the modern merchant increasingly market throwaway products that must be replaced rather than tended to, from the plastic cup to the disposable razor to the telephone answering machine, VCR, or TV that is cheaper to change than to fix. Instead of supplementing our own intellectual and physical powers and skills, new technologies often produce goods that further devalue them, indeed, that depend on our not having on them. Driven by advertising, having something "new" becomes a primary symbol of success, one crucial way to be first. New goods, however, require more money and make insecure, enervating jobs all the more precious. And making more money requires more time.

Where jobs are insecure and sometimes difficult to find, employers can demand overtime and make the workday longer. Jobs not anchored in immediate neighborhoods require more time to reach. The time left for leisure becomes less truly free, as time must be "spent" to advance oneself in one's community or workplace. Women, especially, have less time. Freed from farming chores, they find themselves spending countless hours preparing husbands and children for the economy: shopping, cooking, entertaining, helping with homework, doing household chores, and driving children, it seems, everywhere. As attitudes toward women's work change once again and as wages and salaries go less far, women both work for pay away from home while working without it in the home.

Long hours and commuting time and the need for two breadwinners create other needs for goods and services. New commodities are marketed as ways of dealing with the time crunch, from washing and dishwashing machines to TV dinners to day care, modular phones, home computers, and quick ways to negotiate credit. Many of these create new needs of their own, especially of the time it takes to earn the money to pay for them.

Time becomes the scarcest commodity of all. No wonder the modern age is replete with discussions of time, from how best to use it to how to avoid becoming a procrastinator to how to "have it all."

From within this myth of origin—and especially its belief in a time gone by of more ordered harmonies—modern society is seen as both unnatural and unable to deliver on its promises. Economic growth becomes a euphemism for a rat race that no one can win or escape from. Our choices are clear. We can repudiate the growth society and recreate a more natural world or we can continue to earn and spend simply to cope with our lives.

Paradise Reexamined

Thus ends the ecofundamentalist myth of the origin of modern industrial society, its social and environmental travails, and its current political dilemma—the myth of Paradise Lost. Powerful as this myth is, it leaves its own unanswered questions, has its own gaps, spins its own web of illusions.

There is considerable evidence that much medieval practice, including the charivari and the church confessional, were needed to inscribe the norms of domestic life. The very existence of these practices indicates how much resistance and deviance may accompany an order.

To explore the ecofundamentalist myth, let's begin with the obvious question of why such preindustrial societies with their ordered harmonies would collapse. Polanyi (1957) is correct in pointing to various forms of coercion as a causal agency in, for example, the disruption of the commons that had always sustained such households. Still, the hope for a better life and different world clearly gripped some of these citizens. From what were they escaping? Why, during World War I, was a song featuring the following lyrics so enormously popular: "How are you going to keep them down on the farm, once they've seen Paris?"

Although it may be easy to exaggerate the number of hours and difficulty of work on farms and homesteads, surely such work was physically hard and often dangerous. If today's dependence on an anonymous market is risky, an economy in which one really could only depend on the self, as farmers perhaps knew best, also courted disaster. Therefore, if one can make arguments for relative self-sufficiency and reducing dependence on far-flung markets and experts, is not absolute self-sufficiency purchased at a high price? Illich (1981) and Polanyi (1957) can perhaps evade this question by assuming a bounty and constancy to nature, but these assumptions are as problematic as notions of nature's total manipulability and malleability. Surely even many premodern peoples who experienced droughts, floods, and hurricanes must have had moments of doubt and anxiety about nature's providential bounty.

In addition, the problems are not just lurking economic dangers. For even as modern industrial capitalism disrupted household life, the constraints, anxieties, and inequities of that life itself may have prepared its participants to accept redefined roles and the consumer siren song.

To illustrate, let us look specifically at Ivan Illich's portrait of the self-sufficient farm in the early 19th-century local market economy. He describes a world where men and women engaged in household production of candles, rugs, shoes, animals, and garden vegetables both for their own consumption and for sale to others in local markets. He portrays men and women performing equal though different tasks within the household and being economic equals. One must ask why anyone would want to leave. Yet women as well as men came to seek commodities not easily provided by this world and sought escape to a larger world. Can we confidently assume that, for most of them, the consumption was forced or merely reflected an artificially created status need imported from the outside? Furthermore, if the emerging production and consumption mentality reflected an overweening human hubris, why would the same criticism not apply to early 19th-century villagers'—and Illich's—valorization of these early societies and the nature that sustains them?

Was the move to a broader market simply coerced? If status was the issue, what in the life of the old community made people so insecure?

Illich's (1981) answer has two parts. Like Polanyi (1957), he cites the role of industrial capital in expropriating the commons and making any kind of rural life much less viable. He also acknowledges that this force by itself could not have effected these changes as broadly or completely as it seems to have. He then turns to the role of an emerging patriarchal-capitalist worldview. He remarks, "While men were encouraged to revel in their new vocation, women were surreptitiously redefined as the ambulant, full time matrix of society" (p. 107). We agree that coercion and structural pressures were involved, though even this explanation raises issues as to why homesteads were so vulnerable and whether some of the merchant capital came from the community itself.

Coercion by itself, however, fails to explain why men submitted (and sometimes agreed) to the prospect of working away from home or women agreed to laboring within it. Although modern technologies may have created new social needs, could they not have relieved many women of back-breaking kitchen and laundry chores?[7]

Furthermore, one must wonder if inequalities in power were lodged not only in the community but within the practices of home life even as women enjoyed a substantial role within the preindustrial household in producing goods for home and market. How were the terms of the division of labor in these early households established? Many formal ontologies of premodern thought, from "God the Father" to the limited role of women in the Catholic Church, suggest a clearly subordinate role for women in the elaboration and articulation of basic social practices. Within Protestant theology, man as active agent in transforming the world comes to play a significant theological role with major economic implications.

Are we to assume that these formal ontologies had no significance within these preindustrial homes? Might some women, frustrated by the limitations of male leadership within the domestic arena and yet gripped by a religious worldview and its understanding of man, have seen the new world and its messianic promises as a powerful new dream, however much that dream may have been shaped by the limits of their current situations and understandings? The complicated netherworld where women enjoyed a substantial production role within a home and culture still defined by an active male leadership may itself have been a source of frustration, anxiety, and confusion for both men and women.

For men, one may wonder if part of the attraction of industrial work lay in anxiety about their collaboration with women in a culture whose most powerful religious and political symbolism—especially in a Protestant era—celebrated men as active creators. In the process, the roles of both men and women were redefined; these redefinitions over time became the dominant ones. Nonetheless, however frustrated and limited in options by prevailing ideology and social practice they were, these working-class men and women may be viewed as playing some active part, however subordinate, in this process of change.

Finally, unless overwhelming physical force was involved, which Illich (1981) does not claim, what does it say about women to portray them as manipulated by such an ideological process? Are they by nature powerless or private creatures? Illich's account, like many other analogous tales of social decay, carries the implication of innocent beings removed from paradise through manipulation. But as in Genesis, the first tale of this sort, one must wonder what factors predisposed the corrupted to believe the serpent.

Political theorist Joan Cocks (1989) argues that radical feminists often use an "instrumentalist" view of power that, unwittingly, turns the role of subordinated women into that of innocent victims of men's "original genius." Although the radical view provides the gratification of saying that "they" have done this to "us," Cocks claims "it is a long leap from the claim that a dominant group exerts a tyrannical agency in society to the claim that it exerts sole agency" (p. 182). Both dominant and subordinate exist within a "particular classificatory and practical order" in which

> to the extent that consciousness is mastered, it will be so in the most fundamental sense as a comrade of its dominant counterpart under the same discursive regime, breathing the same ideological atmosphere, which is not to say (in fact, it is to say quite the contrary) that the regime and the atmosphere dictate identical self-images, proclivities, and passions to both parties. (p. 189)

Therefore, she suggests "a new methodological rule of thumb" in the study of power:

> The initial movement one looks to trace is not from outside the bounds of an order of truth in (the sort of movement by which virgin minds are inculcated with hegemonic ideas), but from inside the bounds of that order, where every mind begins, out. (p. 190)

We shall see in subsequent chapters that Cocks's (1989) perspective has applicability beyond contemporary radical feminism. Even within the area of environmental politics, many of the radical critics of contemporary industrialism also tacitly share assumptions with the discursive regime of the political economy they critique. In an analogous fashion, these shared assumptions pose substantial problems for their critique.

In the immediate context, Illich's (1981) portrait of the American home-based economy and its populist culture raises a deeper set of questions. One is struck by internal tensions within attitudes toward markets and competition. Populists celebrate the small firm in the competitive market along with freedom of contract. Even Illich's small farms strive to make money in outside markets. The problems lie in the emergence of large-scale industry and the domination of life by industrial production. One must ask, however, how these larger firms, the ostensible source of the problems identified by populists, emerge. Are they not partly the result of the competitive dynamics and the freedom of contract celebrated in the model? Followers of Andrew Jackson's "democracy" celebrated both the independent farmer and laissez-faire economics. So did many agrarian rebels at the close of the 19th century. Yet did the undermining of one follow from the prizing of the other?

Populism has sometimes invoked the specter of the greedy merchant or, more ominously, the avaricious ethnic type turning to government for political favoritism as one explanation. Historians sometimes paint this mode of thinking as a dark side of populism, which is characteristic only of its declining periods. Populist insistence on direct democracy is surely a great contribution to our political culture. Nonetheless, to see democracy as an instrument and a product of a naturally harmonious and virtuous people is a potential source of problems. It engenders populism's darker sides. The impulse to see a set of values and practices as natural and its people as harmonious occludes important questions. In this case, one must wonder why some merchants become especially greedy. Is such greed not an intensification of tendencies already present in the reigning character type, indeed, in the economic order? Furthermore, in small and well-ordered communities, why would political and economic leadership be so vulnerable to corruption as to allow the disruptions and intrusions in the first place?

It is instructive that many of the opponents of the industrial—and post-industrial—growth society pose as counterexamples not just self-sufficient homesteads but small and primitive communal societies. Polanyi's (1957) extended treatment of Western Malaysian islanders has become the classic of this genre.[8] These critics cite such examples as proof that human beings are not self-seeking by nature; their arguments are often compelling. As we have seen, however, the forms of meaning that such societies provide may also include impositions on people, which sometimes become proximate causes of social change. The emergence of early capitalism itself was not simply imposed but was a political and social response to tensions and frustrations within that order, albeit ones limited by the ideals and practices of the society from which it emerged.

Against some ecofundamentalist readings of primitive traditions, it is useful to counterpose such contemporary work as that of Andrew Ross (1994) on the Polynesians. Ross tries to avoid presenting any one authoritative reading of Polynesian culture. Nonetheless, he presents historical and anthropological reconstructions that lead us to question further the notion of mutually constructed consensual norms in adequately explaining premodern community behavior. Ross's work suggests that Polynesian traditions never were as clearly uniform and consensual as they are often portrayed to be. Doubts, evasions, and expressions of plural interests more routinely find their way into social life than in fundamentalist accounts. For example, even the nonexploitative relation to nature, much celebrated in and about Polynesian culture, can be explained partly in terms of the tribal nobility's preservation of certain valued spoils, such as prized landscapes, for themselves. Intertwined with a cultural premium on harmony with nature, therefore, is a Polynesian style not only of achieving status but also of material self-interest.

Whether in the 19th-century American homestead and farm, the primitive or premodern society, or the technological industrial or postindustrial economic growth society, we find friction and conflicts among community participants. Even the ostensibly unitary ideals of the community may not be as unitary as imagined or may hide substantial conflict. In these things there is little of concern. An important problem does arise when the community suppresses doubts these tensions engender, obscuring the impositions that help constitute the community's professed ideals. The problem deepens when social thinkers also overlook the gaps and illusions in stories of a better life. They then deny a role for politics in admitting inherent tensions, acknowledging doubts, and limiting impositions. To hear the story only through these myths is not to hear about some of the most human problems of all.

From Myth to Politics

Environmental politics seldom acknowledges that it tacitly invokes myths or that it benefits from the structure of a hidden grand narrative. In subsequent chapters, we spell out an alternative analysis, one that may itself be implicated in its own forms of faith, but nonetheless strives to acknowledge this dependence. We believe this perspective sheds light on features shared by most corporate and environmentalist participants in the current debate on economics and sustainability. Then we draw out the political conclusions we take from our readings of the prevalent myths of origin and their limits.

A close examination of corporate sustainability programs, to which we turn in Chapter 2, still harbors in its background a Promethean myth as to the ultimate ability to reshape the environment to human purposes. In Chapter 3, we will examine two widely discussed alternatives to corporate environmentalism, Paul Hawken's ecopopulism and Barry Commoner's social democratic environmentalism. Commoner's efforts might be read as a powerful effort to wed a belief in industrial progress with a faith in the beneficence of nature. Hawken's ecopopulism, while equally optimistic about the possibilities of technologies, seems to derive more sustenance from ecofundamentalist beliefs in the small community and small scale business. Neither author, however, is close to being as indebted to the myth of Paradise Lost as are such authors as Murray Bookchin (1985, 1986), Rudolph Bahro (1986), and Kirkpatrick Sale (1985). We emphasize Commoner and Hawken because their agendas, though not likely to be enacted soon, are a more substantial presence in environmental politics.

The Arcadian tradition has less presence in American life than various Promethean counterparts. Why this is so in an era of great skepticism about current corporate and government practice is a question worthy of attention. Although this lack of presence is surely due in part to the educational and institutional supports for the Promethean sensibility, there may be other reasons worthy of consideration. This myth may fail to have resonance because it is wedded to romantic illusions about small communities, small businesses, and literal self-sufficiency. Although many of us yearn for community, others (sometimes the same citizens) also fear the gargantuan political power perhaps necessary to restore such a past and may also harbor reservations about the intrusiveness of small scale organizations or groups in which we have lived or worked. Lacking a strategy or perspective to handle such ambivalence, many find in some version of the high-technology growth society their only current "default mode."

These Promethean and ecofundamentalist myths—together or in combination—do not provide a way out of the dilemmas they imperfectly illuminate. Both have little clear sense of the public's role and give little guidance as to what to do in the world of existing corporate giants locked in competition for success and survival. Furthermore, they fail to suggest how workers and citizens will respond and fare as competition becomes more intense within an international market. They do not tell us where national, state, and local governments fit in.

Despite their apparent differences, these myths seem to share assumptions on a range of crucial registers. Environmental and political reconstruction may require coming to grips both with similarities and with the gaps and illusions they point to in each other—and those implicit in our own reconstruction, as well.

At a fundamental level, both myths are implicated in respective paradigms that share important similarities of form and theme. Although corporate ecologists portray nature as endlessly manipulable—without danger if we pay attention to production side effects—ecofundamentalist critics suggest that small communities can be designed to maximize their fit with nature. Nature, if not simply manipulable, can be made to be a proper home for us. Both sides make claims to infinite sustainability and both claim to hold the key to future human happiness. The small community with appropriate soft technology, for one, and the postindustrial society trading pollution permits on the electronic superhighway, for the other, are indicative of safe and sound modes of life that also guarantee human satisfaction. Each side believes itself entitled to thoroughgoing political legitimacy.

Both myths share a second structural similarity. According to both, the seeds of discontent within a harmonious and fully satisfying human life are sown from the outside. The media, the bureaucrats, unnecessary products, greedy entrepreneurs, or advertising are to blame. For neither is there an essential discontinuity within nature, both human and nonhuman, nor between humans and the natural world—no unbridgeable gaps, no irreplaceable losses, no homeless remainders. Such a common perspective undergirds the essentially static or apolitical vision implicit in much sustainability literature on each side—and in the environmental debate itself.

This lack of politics is achieved at great cost, however. Democratic politics must play three key roles in an adequate sustainability discourse. First, it must raise the questions posed by ecofundamentalists—to begin to counterbalance the dominance of those on the other side—as to the ways in which our current order may foster more needs than it fulfills. Second, it should reflect on those areas of weakness in that myth to understand more fully the ways in which industrialization and modernization have produced real gains. In the process of asking each of these, the question of the quality of life is directly raised and counterposed both to the notion that it is simply a derivative of endless material growth and the idea that growth is irrelevant to a better world. Third, democratic politics is also the vehicle by which we can best decide how, if destructive forms of production and consumption are being created, this process can be stopped without resorting to overweening state power, retreating to simplistic counterideals whose impositions are not even acknowledged and whose chance of acceptance is, in any case, remote, or waiting until drastic measures of some onerous sort will be taken because it is too late.

We hope that democratic politics construed in this way will have several distinctive features. In exposing omissions within perspectives, as well as noting shared assumptions across them, we may be able to sort out our problems in a way that speaks to our concerns, challenges us to think and probe further, and thereby gives us the confidence to decide. Because democracy draws from the best resources within our culture, it makes decisions we reach more likely to be politically sustainable.

Of course, such politics will not escape myths of its own. It too may have illusions. Nonetheless, as it develops alternatives, democracy always offers the opportunity to point out, and thereby to limit, the inevitable problems caused by—and intrusions implicit in—the confines of its own discourse. Before we refine the contours of such a perspective, however, we now move from this general background to the way—within environmental politics— dominant corporate sustainability programs define the contemporary political agenda.

Notes

1. Although we have attempted no quantitative study of this matter, we suspect that in the realm of advertising, the pastoral outweighs the futuristic in number. Even when the product is the most high-tech product of our society, it is often visually portrayed as a means of returning to an earlier, always simpler, more rural and harmonious world.

2. A compelling theoretical account of the medieval worldview and the changes accompanying the growth of Protestantism and capitalism can be found in Taylor (1985b).

3. State socialists also protest the interference with progress entailed by promoting individual rights, although they root it not in the rights of private property but in the rights of the managers of social property to represent progress itself.

4. Another way would be to develop market mechanisms through government tax policy to reward prodigious procreation. Simon (1985) does not advocate this. It may be entailed in his belief that a competitive economic mentality needs no fettering to restrain the purposes to which it will be put, which implies no role for religion, tradition, culture, or ethics.

5. Rifkin (1995) discusses the role of technology in creating redundant and underpaid labor. Rifkin makes a powerful case for the role of technology change in fostering these problems, but in our eyes underplays the role of corporate power and economic inequality in this process.

6. On the question of predictability in the social sciences, see MacIntyre (1984, chap. 8). MacIntyre also provides a provocative discussion of the role of predictivist models in engendering a certain kind of bureaucratic model and in limiting citizen access to information and opportunity for input.

7. See Strasser (1982) for an excellent discussion of the role of technology in the household. Strasser understands that technology can create new needs but she does not use this consideration to argue against all improvements in household technology or to celebrate the premodern household.

8. Polanyi (1957, pp. 46-47) provides telling evidence that growth and acquisitiveness is not natural or at least no more unable to be guided than any other human propensity. He fails, however, to probe the evident anxieties inside those societies. Why, for instance, are the practices of ostracism that he describes so prevalent? What does this tell us about the social need to maintain norms in these societies or the propensity to violate them?

2 The New Corporate Politics of Sustainability

The Emergence of Environmental Politics

It is fashionable in some environmentalist circles to ridicule commercial promotion of green products or corporate advertisements portraying business as fully committed to the environment. After all, American corporations have long enjoyed much freedom in the introduction of new chemicals into both products and work processes. This freedom was accompanied by few requirements that technology choices be recorded for or available to public scrutiny. Nevertheless, corporate environmentalism is a serious effort to achieve an economically viable solution to environmental problems and a politically palatable solution to environmental issues.

In this chapter, we examine the corporate response to federal efforts to protect the environment. Corporate responses have gone through three stages: (1) indifference to an environmental movement corporations did not understand and the implications of which they did not grasp; (2) efforts to roll back and remove any regulation; and (3) an effort to enact an entirely new regulatory paradigm. Corporate leadership has learned that it can no longer function without an environmental agenda of its own. Nonetheless, corporate programs remain indebted to various forms of Promethean thinking and limited by some of the unresolved dilemmas that flow from this inheritance.

Environmental politics was clearly at the center of the political stage by the late 1960s. From today's perspective, it is striking how little prepared for the demands placed on them corporate leaders were. They were neither too concerned about environmental implications or well mobilized to participate in political discussions. President Richard Nixon, sounding both as determined and as apocalyptic as the staunchest environmental leader, remarked in his 1970 State of the Union message that "the 1970s absolutely must be the years when America repays its debt to the past by reclaiming the purity of its air, its waters, and our living environment. It is literally now or never" (quoted in Commoner, 1990, p. 173). It was he who established the Environmental Protection Agency (EPA) by executive order.

Early environmental legislation gave to the EPA the job of quantifying the risk posed by chemicals regarded as potentially hazardous. Based on the risk determination, the agency could then establish levels thought to be safe and mandate appropriate standards. In some cases, it could also order producers to use the best available technology or compel them to devise new technologies to meet agency requirements.

With regard to the process of setting standards or granting permits to plants for specific emission levels, the statutes mandated public comment and even invited public interest litigation. In the 1970s, the agency set standards for some major industries, including utilities, paper producers, and automobiles. These entailed major changes in technology and sometimes in the final consumer product.

The setting of standards first required accumulation of information, with tests done in instances when the effects of chemicals were relatively unknown. In those areas, tests were carried out and standards were provisionally established, but at this point producers would usually file their own test data and protest the government analysis. Major methodological controversies and large areas of uncertainty in the scientific basis of regulation invited a tug-of-war as to the relative degree of risk. Once determination was made as to the level of risk, technology choices were mandated and an extended comment period and follow-up discussion occurred. The cost of even relatively small advances in environmental quality was high. The very length of the process was expensive for both government and industry and, coupled with the cost and inconvenience of technology change often required of producers, led to intensified political and legal resistance to the standards.

More than a decade after enactment of environmental reform, most reputedly hazardous chemicals had not even been subjected to this process. The statistics on many of the major air and water pollutants that had been evaluated and regulated remained rather bleak. Although the smog over some Eastern cities had abated and some lakes and rivers had been salvaged from the worst forms of industrial pollution, environmental damage remained substantial.

Progress was slow for three related reasons. Control technologies never worked as well as anticipated. The number of sources of pollution grew with the expanding economy, reducing the effectiveness of even high standards. Because many regulations simply imposed one technology choice, they often locked corporations into modes of pollution reduction that soon became obsolete and should have been abandoned.

There was another basic problem with this approach that became apparent over time. Controlling pollution largely by capturing the discharge of noxious compounds begged the question of what to do with the by-products of the control technologies. Disposal of hazardous by-products itself soon became a regulatory nightmare, occasioning the same dynamics of risk assessment and technology imposition. A whole new industry with costs that would be borne largely by the consumer but that also cut into producer profits, time, and freedom was created.[1]

Environmental economist Eban Goodstein (1995) presents a careful and balanced analysis of the gains that have flowed from the "command-and-control" agenda employed to one degree or another during most of the last two decades. His assessment could be taken as a reflection of the frustrations of both corporate and environmental leaders with environmental politics. He remarks that, in spite of a virtual doubling of economic activity between 1970 and 1990, air quality has improved somewhat and water quality has not deteriorated below 1970 standards. Economic growth itself, however, threatens continually to overwhelm whatever gains the regulatory process has achieved. Although each production unit manages to produce a smaller amount of pollution, the total level of pollution remains relatively static.

The regulatory process has had an ambiguous effect on this dynamic. On the one hand, by gathering information and discussing its significance, regulators helped create awareness of environmental problems. Although regulatory procedures may have made implementation slow, they also kept the issue alive. In doing so, they exacerbated the dilemma in which corporations found themselves, while constraining them to take action.

The regulatory process unwittingly also created expectations that it could not fulfill—and it did so in a context of changing political currents and continuing frustrations, not only with the quality of life but with government. It therefore helped position the answer corporate environmentalists could give, but not in a way free of obstacles.

Early environmental politics and the success of corporate resistance occurred during an era of broadening distrust of basic American institutions. The civil rights movement and protests against the Vietnam War were both a backdrop for and a catalyst of environmental politics. For a variety of reasons, citizens were challenging the authority of leadership in government and business.

If the wisdom of introducing unknown technologies into the production process was a concern, so too were outside impositions from government regulators constantly changing the rules. Cynicism about all authority coupled with a top-down environmental strategy helped neutralize the rank and file labor movement's faith in government. This phenomenon became especially pronounced as rates of productivity and job growth slowed within the internationalizing economy, undermining government's ability to deliver the goods. America's relative economic power declined. At the same time, its military was floundering in the Vietnam quagmire. Declining international economic and political power was driven home to the American public in stark fashion with the Arab oil boycott of 1973. By the late 1970s, the United States faced a unique economic phenomenon that became known as *stagflation*: slow growth and prices rising at the same time (see Buell, 1995, chs. 3 and 4).

With the economy in disarray, corporate acquiescence or complacency on environmental issues became short-lived and conservative political interventions more likely to achieve success. The first instinct was to dismantle the whole set of environmental policies. Deregulation became the watchword. Surprisingly, such a strategy was still very problematic. Public environmental fears were never fully displaced even by economic stagnation.

Corporate environmentalism emerged as a reaction to both the economic threat of the prevailing regulatory process and the recognition that unless there was an alternative, political support would go to the government regulators by default. Ignoring environmental problems was no longer an option.

A bold-faced deregulatory momentum was hard for President Ronald Reagan to maintain even at the height of his popularity. Movements toward complete deregulation often tempt business leaders during conservative eras. Unlike attacks on welfare, however, complete reversal of the federal role in the environmental area never became a popular option. The production of wastes continued to create disposal issues, and as soon as the economy began a modest rebound late in Reagan's first term, disposal of toxics and regulation of other modes of production were back at the center of American politics.

Surprisingly, corporate leadership seems to have played some role in this process. Even in the dark days of national environmental politics, local groups, inspired by the example of Love Canal, continued to worry about nuclear, petrochemical, and waste production facilities located or planned for location in their neighborhoods. These so-called "not in my backyard"

(NIMBY) movements had an enormous effect. Besides creating a serious obstacle to industrial development, they generated a fear that localities would develop their own environmental rules. In an effort to preempt the legal space for such regulation while stopping political momentum, some corporate leaders began to articulate a new model of environmental regulation (Dickson, 1984).

Corporate environmentalism has focused on two essential goals. First, it aims to free the economy from that part of chronic stagnation associated with a model of inflexible environmental protection that imposes the same standards or technologies on all producers. Second, it seeks to circumvent the unwillingness of the population either to relax environmental standards or to bear the burdens of controlling environmental hazards.

Free Market Environmentalism

The belief that one can displace public concern about the environment with simple incantations of faith in technology or in the resiliency of nature is largely now dead in corporate circles. One can see in corporate environmentalism, however, a faith that remains subtly indebted to that earlier set of beliefs. Most modern corporate leaders assume that pollution, resources, and toxics can be privately managed in ways that maintain profitability, technological leadership, and environmental integrity in a competitive world economy. Growth can be clean.

The basic method of corporate environmentalism is to incorporate the costs of environmental degradation into the internal costs of production. The goal is to create a competitive environment in which corporations, to succeed economically, must choose the most cost-effective ways to avoid damaging the environment. In establishing the level of regulatory actions, however, market principles are also to dominate: The costs of regulation are to be weighed against the monetary value of its benefits.

The corporate response has focused on two areas: point of production regulation and hazardous waste management. In both, the market model predominates. Corporate leadership has been especially critical of the technology mandating aspects of conventional regulatory approaches. Goodstein (1995) points out that in many command-and-control regulatory schemes, existing plants were "grandfathered," thereby creating a bias against constructing new, more efficient and potentially less polluting facilities. In addition, any specific control technology may not be the most appropriate for all parts of the country. More fundamentally, once a mandated technology is in place, there is no incentive to seek control devices that might be more beneficial and efficient. The greatest claimed advantage of free market environmentalism, therefore, is that it does not lock in existing technology nor does it mandate who should make reductions. It allows both cost-effective technological innovation and economically efficient environmental protection.

Gretchen Morgenson and Gail Eisenstodt (1990) summarize the corporate environmentalist position on environmental degradation. They comment that citizens are the primary cause of pollution

> because we want convenient products and we want them cheap. We want low jet fares and safe and comfortable cars, and we want to be able to toss away our toddlers' diapers, drink soft drinks from light weight plastic jugs. We live in a world of relative leisure because energy consuming products do so much work for us. (p. 97)

Morgenson and Eisenstodt claim that one of the worst sources of water pollution, for example, is not large plants but the use of labor-saving fertilizer and pesticides by thousands of individual farmers. The way to deal with the by-products of our perpetual quest for more convenient and cheaper goods is to establish reasonable standards for pollutants and then place a sufficiently high tax on those to reach that standard. They believe that such an approach is much better than substituting

> the actions of a relatively small number of bureaucrats for the actions of tens of millions of freely acting individuals and so lose the market's stunning ability to harness a great deal of information. Moreover, if individual consumer choice is circumvented, abuse of the political system grows. The peoples of Eastern Europe have spent half a century learning this. Californians may spend the next half century learning it. (p. 96)

Fortunately, residents of California may not need to wait half a century to try the free market approach to sustainable economics. President Bill Clinton's Earth Day speech of 1994 called for "less bureaucracy, regulation, or unnecessary cost," in part to liberate the corporate sector (quoted in Ginsberg, 1994, p. 23). At least some of the thrust of such an approach was embodied in the Clean Air Amendments of 1990. Under regulations employing one well-developed form of this model, utilities and other industrial firms can trade the right to discharge certain amounts of noxious compounds into the air. If one firm has a technology or plant that allows it to reduce pollution more cheaply than another, it will sell its right to pollute to that other facility.

In this way, a form of environmental comparative advantage can emerge. Each firm specializes in what it does best and the economy as a whole achieves high levels of pollution control with the least sacrifice in goods and services.

Genteel Laissez-Faire

In the abstract, it is hard to fault such a model, just as it is hard to criticize the classical paradigm from which it is drawn. Nonetheless, as with the classical model, the notion of markets producing self-perpetuating and socially optimizing equilibria is, in part, a form of faith. One may wonder, for instance, whether the normal competition of firms in an economy will not make some players much larger, limiting the extent to which the market is really free. Would not the market in pollution shares be subject to similar tendencies? The strongest firms might be able to drive up prices, thereby making it more difficult for weaker and more polluting competitors to modernize. Indeed, the very complexity that may attend such trading could work to the advantage of the larger firms. Free market economists themselves have commented on the ways regulation in our market economy often works to the advantage of the stronger.

The environment is even less easily understood as one market. Prevailing winds make certain areas of the country receptors of effects from decisions made in other places. The purchase of pollution permits by several Midwestern utilities may mean that some Eastern cities and towns will now receive very large concentrations of noxious compounds, whereas other areas escape pollution entirely. In addition, many affected communities may not even be part of the trading system. Even within states and regions, pollution is heavily concentrated in certain areas. It is possible that some plants, especially older ones more likely to purchase pollution shares rather than to install new control devices, will be located in such areas. Further discharges may make these areas even more unlivable.

If the choices are to be made by a regulatory arm of the federal government or the states—that is, made politically—choosing between these areas will be extremely difficult and bitterly contested. Part of the political appeal of free market environmentalism lies in its attempt to find a smooth and easy "economic" way to answer questions such as this, especially on the issue of inequity between regions.

Advocates of the market model claim as a primary virtue (and hold as an assumption) the idea that markets do not concentrate power per se. They regard the political process, if needed at all, as simply assuring the continuity and legality of self-regulating markets. The assumption is that the process will, therefore, not be compromised by power imbalances.

There is a fundamental reason, however, why politics and power can never really be exorcised from the process this model attempts to describe. Some individual or group or institution must set the initial price of the permits, determine the number that will be issued, and set the criteria of damage assessment to be used to determine price and number. Or decide on the kind and extent of tax to place on offending products or polluters. Or write the property and torts law on which civil damage suits will be litigated.

The question of damage is assumed to be relatively straightforward on the theory that natural phenomena can be fully understood. Even when damage is not clear, free market environmentalism assumes that fair venues for the determination of these questions exist in the minimal administrative state and the law. If, however, any economic interest is able to gain an advantage—and free market theorists expect every actor to try to do so—why would it not use the political arena to enforce that advantage through the process of standard setting? Indeed, this is precisely the criticism free market environmentalists level at the administrative state: Its regulators themselves develop self-interests.

Consider the experience with the process of setting standards for pollutants. In the early years of environmental regulation, legislators generally used language that suggested an uncompromising concern for public safety. At the administrative level—especially in recent years—that concern has often been compromised by industry-backed efforts to limit regulations through the imposition of controversial cost-benefit standards.

Because the field of toxicity studies is far from an exact science, agencies are swamped with competing factual and methodological claims. Reagan's deregulatory initiatives succeeded in cutting back on the availability of the kind of independent government scientific expertise needed to analyze test data. The EPA sometimes finds itself turning to consultants whose main income derives from work on behalf of chemical companies. Initial test data often come from these same companies. In a context of conflicting information and diminishing government sources, the role of lobbyists becomes substantial. All these trends undermine the faith of the public in the government's ability to protect them.

It is also hard not to see other ethical and political problems in the process of risk assessment. Part of the damage of any pollutant often is the loss of human life. Because the goal of free market environmentalism is to foster safety by factoring all costs into the production process, one must put a market price on all aspects of environmental damage. Advocates of this model, therefore, must come up with a figure for the loss of human life. One method of quantifying such a concept is to estimate the wages an individual would receive during a specified period of his or her life and to use this figure as the basis for the value of that life. Another method is to assess how much of a wage premium must be paid to an individual to assume jobs with higher than ordinary chances of death. Such approaches of course assume the equity of the market's wage and salary determination. They also treat human life as simply one commodity among others.

Although this procedure has drawn much criticism, less attention has been given to the reasons this approach has gained such prominence. The use of market-based monetary value of human life to determine the strictness of environmental and safety standards removes from politics the question of the importance society places on material economic growth. It displaces the question of how much preservation of life really means to us and if we are willing to adjust present growth patterns or future scenarios to fulfill this meaning.

The emergence of corporate environmentalism, then, is partly explained as an effort to divorce regulatory efforts from this larger issue. It is perhaps not accidental that it took root at a time when growth was stalled or slowed and a substantial segment of the population felt its economic well-being threatened. The public was therefore less likely to accept any interference with market-led growth but it still remained concerned with environmental risks. What better way to resolve this dilemma than to promise an apolitical scientific and market agenda that would balance growth and risk?

One might argue, however, that if a society could foster economic and health security for all its citizens and reduce the burden of work, it might choose to spend more than the cost of a human life—as measured by lifetime wages—to save lives perceived at risk. Worse still, as a range of ecofundamentalists and other critics claim, society may be trapped by cultural and institutional commitments to modes of unfulfilling growth that may even degrade life's quality. In either case, market prices would be sending signals worthy of political examination and possible contestation. Allowing bureaucratic experts to place a one-time value on human life simply removes these important questions from the broader moral and political debate they merit.

Cost-benefit analysis, as often practiced, is not free of other ethical implications worth probing. Like environmental hot spots, costs and benefits are often concentrated. For example, a regulation may save only a few lives in certain communities and at a relatively large cost. The conclusion might be not to regulate. But what if these communities are already burdened by high levels of poverty, toxics, and dangerous illnesses? Is there a point at which certain groups should not be asked to bear any more costs? Can these issues be settled in a just fashion simply through application of cost-benefit techniques?

Should we also assume that all people are affected in the same way by the discharge of pollutants—that is, the cost is the same per person? What if those who have better access to health care and education are also able to achieve earlier detection and faster response to potential health problems? The cost to their health is likely to be less, but this consideration is not factored into conventional cost-benefit calculations.

The corporate environmental program elides such ethical and practical questions with the assumption that markets assure adequate individual opportunities to choose benefits and escape disproportionate incidence of costs. Indeed, it assumes that the greater efficiency of its model will lead to more job creation, which will benefit the unemployed. Old plants in relatively undesirable neighborhoods may be the ones that buy the right to pollute and choose to defer long-term capital improvement. Over time, a lack of economic competitiveness may force them to cut back or go out of business entirely. Will more efficient plants in other neighborhoods or a market need for workers to develop control technologies take up the slack in jobs? Even if the total number of jobs remains the same, relocation of jobs places burdens on those who must migrate with the jobs or to whom the jobs become geographically out of reach. Pollution control in this model derails the benefits of economic growth for those in most need of it.

Finally, corporate environmentalism is not free of the kinds of administrative problems often associated with regulatory agencies. For example, monitoring pollution trading arrangements can become burdensome in ways reminiscent of regulations in the command-and-control systems. The very technological innovation in production these systems are supposed to stimulate may make monitoring even more difficult. These problems become even more extreme when the primary sources of pollution are so-called nonpoint or mobile sources, as seems increasingly to be the case in many areas. In some instances, relevant pollution monitoring technologies have not yet even been developed. Advocates of tradable entitlements for Southern California, for example, are concerned about how to develop technologies that will monitor the range of airborne chemicals produced in furniture manufacturing.

The problem of monitoring compliance in any environmental regulatory regime is one to which advocates of corporate environmentalism are not oblivious. Yet, corporations' urge to solve these problems within the terms of the neoclassical free market paradigm is part of the problem. The goal is cost-effective regulation that is as unintrusive as possible. As some acknowledge, however, cost-effective regulation requires frequent inspection of repeat offenders, fines to foster compliance, and strategic decisions as to whether these will be more effectively carried through by juries or by administrative officers. Such difficulties may be necessary consequences of any environmental program. Indeed, free market environmentalists have proposed some ideas that should be considered useful tools, but these ideas are far from a panacea. For example, relying solely on monetary or punitive deterrents may reproduce the cost-averting behavior that leads to the evasion of environmental protections in the first place.

Alternatively, strategies that emphasize participation in the formulation of environmental rules and equalization of their burdens might help facilitate the emergence of environmental values. They might foster the sense of responsibility as well as peer pressure that would lessen the initial urge to violate the norms. This kind of approach is, however, completely outside the conventional corporate agenda.

Other similarities between the corporate neoliberal program and the older-style liberal regulatory one exist. Even the neoliberal agenda must face the question of what to do with the by-products of its modes of pollution control. In this case, less "costly" techniques that remove a pollutant from general circulation are rewarded. These may involve the creation of new wastes, which can be much smaller in volume but are perceived to be, or are, very toxic. Where do these wastes go?

Here, as in the command-and-control approach, free market environmentalism must turn to the construction of hazardous waste facilities, which are regulated according to the same principles of cost-benefit analysis. Administrators establish the level of risk and then issue regulations appropriate to that level. Risk assessment here is just as problematic as in the conventional command-and-control agenda, however. As with every step on this ladder, scientific uncertainty plays a major role and the question of whose science is to be believed comes up repeatedly. In addition, someone must decide what the risks are and what level of such risks are acceptable.

The Tragedy of the Commoners

The hope of corporate environmentalists is that their model gives everyone an economic stake in a clean environment. Indeed, the reigning metaphor of this school is the tragedy of the commons; it bears close examination. The metaphor helps sustain and in turn is sustained by the broader Promethean myth discussed in Chapter 1.

The tragedy of the commons asserts that a private stake in a resource, whether land, timber, air, or water, is the only means by which to assure responsible care of it. The background assumption is that because humans are self-interested beings, we take responsibility only for what we own. The classic statement is Garrett Hardin's famous essay (1977) in which he argues that common ownership of such resources as pasture land led to their destruction. Each rancher tried to get the most out of the pasture before fellow ranchers did the same. It was in everyone's self-interest to take what they could and in no one's self-interest to protect the commons. The solution is to replace the commons with private ownership of the land the commons formerly comprised. Morgenson and Eisenstoldt (1990) draw on this metaphor in asserting that public land management is the reason for the "mess" much of the public lands are in:

> The trouble with public or common ownership of lands is that because no one really owns them, no one has a stake in keeping that property from deteriorating. Land that is generally tended to and cared for generally increases in value, so when property is privately held, incentives to maintain its beauty are strong. When the government is the owner, these incentives disappear. (p. 100)

This view, harnesses the very acquisitiveness its own practices help to sustain as a defense of this model itself. Such lack of self-reflection occludes other "natures" we also have and may put to good use. Hardin, in other words, makes these ways of being in the economic world seem normal. He "naturalizes" them. Hardin and his advocates assume that a certain kind of acquisitive and possessive behavior is natural and not in need of explanation. No one will care about land that he or she does not own. In addition, they assume that there are only two models of administration of the commons. Either the commons must be owned privately or it must be administered by a large government bureaucracy. They fail to acknowledge that there may be a difference between a commons, an area generally frequented by a group that shares common social, cultural, and religious experiences, and an area to which randomly associated individuals have open access.

Hardin and his followers imagine no model of joint management, for example, in which individuals have the opportunity through interaction, education, or participation to demonstrate or to develop a sense of responsibility to each other and to common resources. Instead, their model fears the very view of human nature fixed in and yet also promoted by that model. This may not be the only comprehensive perspective on resource use.

Some researchers who have studied such models both historically and in a variety of so-called Third World settings argue that commons are managed at least as well through cooperative arrangements as through private ownership. Martin O'Connor (1994b) reports that in New Zealand, Maori tribes have carefully managed their own local fisheries without staking out any private claims to them. Poaching and exploitation are results of high-technology foreign intrusions, in this case fishing boats, whose goal is to maximize profits rather than to preserve the fishery as part of a traditional way of life. For the Maori, the fisheries are integral to a common way of life; preservation of that way of life is basic to Maori identity. That way of life, in turn, is constituted by and makes possible a set of reflexively shared values. A tradition is valuable to a person because it ties him or her to others through common bonds—the bonds embodied in the tradition. Although one should not romanticize the Maori culture, or any premodern community (see discussion of Polanyi in Chapter 1), it is hard to see these ways of life as leading inevitably to the natural resource exploitation feared by Hardin (1977).

More modern communities also are constructed on shared values. Too often, however, these values frame forms of interaction that carry a high environmental price tag. These societies have the important virtues of valuing political community, joint decision making, and self-consciousness of one's role in creating traditions. In addition, they are economically productive. These differences from traditional societies hold out the hope that we can reconstitute our values and practices to conform with other less destructive parts of our own traditions or to begin to develop new ones. In doing so, we may be able jointly to manage the commons in ways unimaginable in Hardin's analogy—that is, if we ourselves don't become obsessively tradition bound.

In any case, the solution Hardin endorses, privatization of the commons, may actually exacerbate the primary problem he wishes to solve: that of the free rider. Free riders are citizens who benefit from widespread social practices or norms, but who can get away with few or no contributions to their maintenance. If humans are essentially acquisitive and possessive, as Hardin (1977) supposes, why should they obey newly posted boundaries? Isn't it in my interest to steal from my neighbor unless I am afraid I will be caught? Such a mind-set is most likely to occur in settings in which citizens have little voice in devising property systems and substantial inequalities emerge, leaving some citizens with little if any property and even less understanding of the norms on which property is built. Or it occurs in situations in which success is measured only by the accumulation of wealth.

Property is not, however, an obvious phenomenon existing in some prepolitical state of nature, as for John Locke (discussed in Kuehls, 1996). It is a complex and changing bundle of rights and obligations that emerges within a culture and has always been subject to political, legal, and sometimes extralegal contestation. Hardin falls back on the hope that a culture that respects private property will prevail and its traditions will gird his call for privatization. The behavior he expects is not as "natural" as he makes it out to be after all.

Success for privatization in environmental matters may require practices that go beyond narrowly self-interested considerations. For example, private ownership of agricultural assets can lead to adequate protection of topsoil and other resources. Where it has done so, however, it has been within cultural expectations about mutual assistance and responsibilities and legal requirements regarding forms of incorporation and patterns of inheritance.

For those who have less faith than Hardin in the equity available from the market—as it often has worked historically—there is the worry that a privatized commons may exclude some citizens from prevailing property systems. When small farms become absorbed into agribusiness, many farmers become dispossessed. These people, in turn, may lose working knowledge of or respect for traditional norms of property exchange.

The process through which agribusinesses and the industries that support them grow is also environmentally instructive. One can point to a picture of large and integrated petrochemical and oil companies devising new products for large farming concerns, withholding rather than disseminating information and influencing government agriculture research priorities. The large petrochemical firms promote modes of research and government subsidy that lead to the use of products they can produce cheaply and market effectively. These research programs may develop, for example, bovine growth hormone and a range of genetically engineered products rather than less marketable forms of natural pest control and organic fertilizers. Once such priorities are in place and the products have been adopted by large commercial farms, other farmers must adopt the environmentally harmful but agriculturally productive techniques or be driven out of business.

Advocates of pure laissez-faire economics do see the specific ways in which government subsidy can distort markets and sometimes deplore them as a corruption of the system brought on by evil politicians. Nevertheless, can they properly portray such actions as external to the system? Could these subsidies be a result of the process of power concentration occurring within markets and extending beyond them into government, politics, and law?

Corporations in collaboration with large agribusinesses seem to foster a range of subsidy policies that stimulate investment in high-tech agriculture. These in turn displace many independent farmers and make many others hired hands on others' land. For the corporation, land is simply a capital asset to be depreciated as long as equal or better investment opportunities present themselves (Strange, 1988). Farm land's value as a place for generations of families, as open space, or even as an aesthetic experience to be enjoyed by nearby residents is not part of the equation. The evolution of property systems frequently fails to have the effect desired by Hardin.

As for the hired workers on such land, they are likely to care less than before about the fate of the land on which they work and less yet about their neighbors. In addition, within work settings where they are regarded simply as a cost of operation, hired workers may be forced to work in a fashion that is dangerous both to themselves and to their surroundings.

Work by economist David Vail (1989) on comparative forestry and agricultural practices in the United States and in social democratic societies suggests that one cannot easily dissociate resource economics from socioeconomic relations. Stumpage prices, the amount paid for unprocessed logs, can be affected by the number of buyers and sellers in a market and their mode of collaboration or competition. With only a few large commercial purchasers of felled logs, collaboration among the giants can keep prices low, leaving loggers with little incentive and few funds to practice conservation practices.

In some contexts, the farm or forest itself becomes a profit center, a fungible asset whose resources will be converted into capital as rapidly as possible if higher rates of return can be attained through other investments. Whether farmers or loggers work on a piece rate system or have secure conditions of employment and real input into their work process also affects their degree of care for the integrity of the forest or farm. So too do governmental commitments regarding research, regulatory, and subsidy policy.

The same sort of analysis applies equally to much public land management. Many public lands are mismanaged. The public bureaus charged with forestry management—especially in the Western United States—have often acted out of concern for the immediate needs of timber companies. These companies have sought a ready supply of cheap logs to ship to low-labor-cost mills abroad (Foster, 1992). Rather than attack such practices by fostering more sustainable forestry, reforming international trade practices, and encouraging a domestic wood processing industry, government policy seems trapped by a trade-off between creating jobs by opening more forests and protecting the forest. Current policy probably destroys more jobs than a more sustainable approach would. Nonetheless, environmentalists' objections to the damage rampant timber cutting does to such species as the spotted owl are met by media reports of war between the owl and the working logger in the West. It would be more correct to argue that the privatization mania has led to a "tragedy of the commoners" along with a tragedy of the environment (Goldman, 1993).

Private Politics

Much of the urge to privatize services basic to production and, indeed, to all economic activity can be seen as a reaction to the failure of earlier regulatory activities and to the fiscal crisis of government at all levels. The lack of good public service in areas such as education, garbage, and transit, for example, leads many citizens to seek private remedies. Privatization also grows out of a problematic reading of U.S. economic history.[2] Public support for private economic development has always been important to the success of private companies; many historic figures, such as Alexander Hamilton, forthrightly conceived it so. The public subsidy of canals and railroads, along with support for pure and applied research, for example, were crucial in creating a context that allowed private firms to grow and thrive.

The urge to privatize, however, like the regulatory effort that preceded it, is an attack on symptoms rather than causes. In many cases, costs are saved not by greater efficiency of services but by turning to nonunionized, private sector workers (Bradley, 1994). Rather than trying to reduce the costs of public service through reforms of the public service workplace or by improving citizen access to the bureaucracy, one simply cuts wages. In the process, one also undermines the incentive for good public service. Costs of such privatization may also be subject to inflation in a context in which a few highly specialized firms may come to dominate local or national markets.

Specifically, how will privatization affect that aspect of the tragedy of the commons implicated in toxic waste disposal? Those who accept privatization as a panacea believe that the complex job of waste transportation, storage, and disposal must be undertaken by private firms so that competition in the market can assure the most efficient achievement of this task.

Taking advocates of this position at their word, however, shouldn't one assume that these private firms would be interested in using the least cost inputs while deriving the highest possible price? Will not public authority have to monitor performance, either through periodic examinations or through licensing, which raises questions privatization was supposed to answer? Is the operation efficient? Who will determine adequate standards of performance? If this determination must be made by government, might this responsibility not corrupt the political processes? Why would firms with so much at stake not be above bribing inspectors? Why should inspectors be above accepting a bribe? What kind of law and police powers are necessary to guard against this corruption?

The dilemmas of relying entirely on private solutions to critical public problems become even more severe as the urge to privatize moves to the subject of finding suitable burial sites for toxic by-products. Consider what happens if too few communities want the economic "benefits" of accepting toxic waste facilities. Privatization advocates have suggested that such facilities be auctioned off, with facility owners continually upping monetary and other promises until a community accepts the offer. Many community advocates argue that such auctions are themselves inherently unfair. Communities do not come to the auction in an equal state: Some are so desperate they may be lured by inadequate compensation.

As a whole, sustainability programs that seek to preserve environmental quality solely through the application of market principles, wittingly or not, often serve to legitimize future patterns of unsustainable growth. The equity of these programs and the claim that they will minimize intrusions in our lives are self-evident only if we unreflectively accept the faith in unregulated markets on which they are premised.

A Future for Corporate Environmentalism

The media often characterize many citizens today as moderately conservative. Yet some citizens seem to regard environmental policy as a process of displacement of the costs of environmental harm from one geographic area or social group to another. Some groups live in areas already subject to obvious environmental damage. Others (or perhaps the same groups) live in areas where future toxic waste facilities are likely to be situated. In most cases, regardless of ideology, citizens oppose this displacement. Increasingly citizens are also coming to understand that the cleanup of one medium creates wastes in the form of another. Current approaches to air pollution, for instance, require capturing toxic wastes that must be disposed of. The whole process of displacing costs across groups seems endless and is one source of cynicism and despair.

It is unsurprising, therefore, that communities resist disposal in their backyards even as there are concomitant efforts to combat this resistance. Andrew Szasz (1994) points out that as facility siting became more difficult in the 1980's, some policy analysts began to advocate a strategy of siting in communities that are least capable of politically resisting . . . recently there has been a flurry of attempts to site hazardous waste facilities on Native American land. (p. 108)

This process of cost displacement has not been limited to national borders. Harvard professor and current Treasury official Lawrence Summers, for example, suggests exporting some of the most offensive wastes to the Third World, arguing that many of these nations were "underpolluted." It would make sense for them to accept pollution in return for compensation. He argues, "I think the economic logic behind dumping a load of toxic waste in the lowest wage country is impeccable and we should face up to that" (quoted in Goodstein, 1995, p. 177).

Perhaps Summers thinks the levels of health enjoyed by many of these nations are so bad that compensation for pollution storage might make them better off. These solutions beg a series of questions. Why have our technologies produced so much toxic material? Why are poor nations, just like poor communities in this country, in such dire economic straits that they might consider such an offer? Within these countries, might the weakest and the least healthy be forced to suffer the ill effects of these wastes while the affluent derive even more prosperity from the compensation for disposal? Are these really solutions to the environmental problems associated with economic growth in both North and South and solutions to the poverty of the South? Are no other production technologies available for economic growth? These questions, no less than Summers's proposal, indicate that the contemporary corporate environmental program is taken from much too limited a menu.

Even the most disadvantaged groups in both the North and the South, however, have resisted—more or less successfully—the process of cost displacement. Success often depends on the level of economic development, turns in the business cycle, the power of the interests wishing to displace costs, and the openness of the political process. In this country, at least, resistance at the community level may suggest that imputed political conservatism is perhaps better understood as skepticism toward inept or intrusive government bureaucracies. Indeed, these usually assert their influence from above and are often unresponsive to the needs of local communities. The EPA is caught between a rock and a hard place. Strong regulation hurts economic growth and jobs. Weak regulation hurts the environment. The EPA thus easily ends up a target of both environmentalists and workers. As a result, regulation gets a bad name. It hurts job growth and it fails to deliver efficient gains in public safety or confidence.

Community resistance to hazardous production technologies or toxic sites also indicates a lack of faith in markets. The real need seems to be to expand the range of choices beyond free market environmentalism on the one hand and intrusive government regulations on the other. This can be accomplished only through a consideration of a broader notion of democratic politics.

For the time being, community resistance to new industrial development has become a major part of the cost of doing business. Corporate leaders must factor substantial lobbying and public relations expenses into many major projects. These costs in turn further increase the prices of many consumer items, placing further legitimacy strains on the political and economic systems.

One response is to turn to new means to isolate environmental and economic decisions from any form of democratic input or resistance. However unlikely, this could entail a more authoritarian political state and probably even more limitations of democratic liberties than those entailed by the current economy and administrative state structure. Alternatively, the same effect could be achieved in more subtle ways by extending the legal definition of property rights and limiting the rights of individuals and groups to litigate for environmental protection with regard to them. Whatever government does, however, one can anticipate continued resistance in some form as long as marketers or regulators impose undesirable solutions on communities.

Free market environmentalists thus share with neoclassical economists the faith that economic growth is the only way to solve problems. Economically it eases poverty. Environmentally it makes sustainability programs efficient. In this perspective, pollution problems become side effects we accept and must control for otherwise desirable ends. Because progress is natural and its dividends are fairly distributed, it is rational to accept unreflectively the dictates of this dominant model of economic growth.

From a differing perspective, environmental problems are indissolubly connected to the nature of growth itself as currently constituted. This is a proximate cause of legitimacy problems regarding either the government's or the market's ability to solve them. A better way to solve these legitimacy problems is to allow communities to play a greater role not just in the politics of environmental regulation but in decisions about the form and content of economic growth itself.

Present corporate priorities, on the whole, do more than prevent a better marriage of ecology and technology. As we elaborate more fully in Chapter 3, they also promote a culture of "shop and spend" that puts extra pressure on the political economy's ability to control the environmental problems it creates. Its modus operandi leads to despair that we can ever reconcile economic and environmental goals and thus calls into question the legitimacy of the whole political economy.

The use of incentive-based regulation should be a part of a constructive and cost-effective sustainability program. The corporate environmentalists are persuasive when they suggest that imposition of solutions without building broader incentives for businesses is an inefficient and ineffective way to achieve environmental safety. In addition, as we argue in Chapter 6, cost-benefit analysis in some form could play a role in environmental politics by establishing which environmental programs offer the promise of saving the most lives with whatever amounts society is willing to commit to this purpose.

Markets are useful tools, but they cannot by themselves solve our environmental dilemmas. As we argue in Chapter 3, they often fail to build sufficient long-run incentives for developing and deploying sustainable technologies. Markets themselves can also concentrate power in ways that not only foster injustice but become barriers to cost effectiveness itself. These points are exemplified in the politics of toxic wastes. The viability of many current pollution-control strategies depends on keeping the cost low by removing the wastes captured and locating them in less well-off communities. The real long-run cost to the nation as a whole is obscured but not eliminated.

Perhaps the most basic inadequacy of corporate environmentalism lies in the assumption that just as markets will provide the efficient allocation of resources, so will they assure full employment of all willing workers and a fair distribution of the fruits of production in accord with everyone's talents and interests.

Labor markets, however, do not always work in the same way that other markets do.[3] The process of economic competition—especially from uneven starting points—often leads to a concentration of the ownership of assets and productive capacity. Large-scale corporations can become productive and generate high profits, but there is no guarantee that these profits will be recycled into further job-creating investments. If incomes lag behind profits, reductions in consumption may follow, in turn putting pressure on profits themselves. The incentive to invest may decline and joblessness may grow.

The traditional Keynesian approach has been to use tax and spend policy to ease underconsumption and create economic growth as conventionally defined. This form of growth is a significant source of some of our environmental problems, however. Joblessness, inequality, growth, and the environment are all interrelated concerns in modern economies.

Are there other ways to generate economic growth and jobs without creating similar environmental dilemmas? Do policies exist that achieve such objectives while being responsive to concerns about the intrusiveness of government or the inadequacies of earlier liberal tax and spend programs?

We must reexamine the ways in which markets not only produce externalities but also shape the content of growth itself. Such an examination suggests that markets are human constructs. Like all our tools, they have their purposes and limitations. Simply regarding them as all-encompassing solutions to all problems does two things. It helps obscure the specific circumstances in which they actually function as intended—that is, as genuinely free markets—and it gets in our way of subjecting them to continuing debate and reexamination through democratic politics and decision making as to what their best uses are.

As we show in Chapter 3, the problem of critical self-examination is not unique to free market environmentalists. It also places important conceptual and political limits on a range of critiques of contemporary environmental policy.

Notes

1. Who bears the cost of increased environmental regulation depends in large part on the nature of consumer demand for particular products. In cases where demand is relatively inelastic, producers can pass much of the cost on to consumers.

2. For a powerful defense of the role of industrial policy even in the 19th century, see Best (1990).

3. A discussion of the ways in which labor markets differ from other markets and of various recession and depression scenarios in modern capitalism can be found in Bowles and Edwards (1993). The authors make clear that labor is not just a cost of production but also a source of demand for the products of the modern firm. Cutting labor's cost, wages, does not necessarily increase demand for labor.

3 The Limits of Ecopolitics

The Rise of Antitoxic Politics

Citizens at the state and local level have strongly mobilized against the use of their communities as sites for toxic waste disposal. The media sometimes foster a perception of these groups as narrowly parochial. These groups are denigrated as being willing to accept the fruits of industrial affluence—as long as they do not pay the costs. These are the groups whose actions provoked Henry Fairlie's (1986) anger because, in his terms, they are helping create economic gridlock.

For those who read material acquisitiveness as at least in part a socially constructed imperative rather than as a natural human propensity, there are other ways of looking at the actions of the "not in my backyard" (NIMBY) groups. When the media single these groups out for self-interested behavior, this portrait obscures the degree to which their behavior is shaped by dominant economic factors. To the extent that their actions are purely self-interested, in what ways are their motivations any different from the corporations Simon (1985) and Fairlie (1986) celebrate? Are they not simply interested in getting good return on their investments in their homes and communities?

Other readings of these movements are possible. Some recent studies suggest that these movements, more than others, have broken with conventionally acquisitive patterns. Communities that rise up in rebellion against siting of waste disposal facilities are often initially motivated by an interest in their immediate surroundings. In the course of these protests, however, many also quickly become concerned about broader social issues, including

48

those of the nature of industrial organization. Political participation broadens their horizons further, making them aware of the kinds of forces arrayed against them. What often begins as fear for one's own community and moves on to resistance to additional unfair burdens leads to an enlarged conception of where one's interests lie, now to include all people in similar circumstances. Just as these activists do not want their community to be polluted, so they are concerned about the use of other communities as toxic burial cites. As Andrew Szasz (1994) suggests, if one must give these groups a tag line, it should be "not in anyone's backyard" (p. 80). Szasz points out that this resistance is grounded in long-standing American reform traditions. These people understand American history as "a struggle of the small people against big government and big business" (p. 81).

Part of these activists' antipathy to the location of toxic dumps in their communities is a sense that these facilities threaten the very purpose that growth purportedly serves—the ability both to establish and to preserve a home and community life. Indeed, one of the reasons activist agitation on this subject is so successful is the immediate connection of toxic discharges to the uncertainties and problems such discharges would inject into home and community. Residents regard these not as simply investments or physical spaces, but as the locus of human activity and commitments. Moreover, many working-class Americans regard the home as a primary form of security for the next generation. Their children's happiness provides an important anchor of meaning in a world in which life's purposes often seem insecure.

Green Market Environmentalism

The growth of grassroots toxic movements has spurred a sympathetic response on the part of some business leaders. Perhaps the most well known of these is Paul Hawken, whose book, *The Ecology of Commerce* (1993), has been the subject of many forums and conferences on sustainable development.

Like the indigenous radical voices who are one part of his audience, Hawken (1993) worries about big government and big business and is committed to local economic development as a central value. He is appalled at the superficial nature of the response to environmental problems on the part of many corporate leaders. He points to the chemical giant Monsanto, which has pledged to cut its emissions of toxics by 90%. Laudable as this goal is, Hawken deems it inadequate because it substantially displaces costs across media. The products Monsanto markets, such as pesticides, foster substantial problems where they are used. Many of the resources drawn on to make them are finite.

For Hawken (1993), the real costs of particular industrial processes are caused not only by discharges from the smokestack or the drainpipe—even if taxes on these succeed in decreasing toxic emissions. One must look at long-term damage done by displacement of pollutants to other media (e.g., the conversion of air pollution to various forms of toxic sludge, as discussed in Chapter 2) and at the relative scarcity of resources. If many suppliers have access to adequate present-day sources in a competitive environment, the present price of resources may not reflect impending scarcity until it is too late to make major structural and economic changes. Taxing outputs in ways that reflect only immediate damage does not fully address these problems.

Instead, Hawken (1993) advocates a broad life-cycle approach to product production and design. Everything that is used to make a product, as well as by-products of the production of the product, must be reusable, as far as possible, in the production of future products.

Hawken (1993) would employ two major policy tools toward this purpose. Life-cycle regulations would require that every manufacturer be responsible not only for all forms of packaging and tools of production but for the product as well—from cradle to grave. Thus even manufacturers of major durable goods such as televisions and refrigerators would be required to reuse or recycle the basic frames of such products.

Hawken (1993) also believes that the technologies on which industry relies are fundamentally flawed—either because they rely too heavily on finite resources or because they cannot be deployed in ways that minimize toxic by-products. To remedy these defects, he proposes a major change in the U.S. tax system. Rather than taxing wages and profits, he would move toward taxes on undesirable forms of technology choice. He believes his system of green fees will "provide powerful incentives to revise and constantly improve methods of production, distribution, and consumption" (p. 171).

Hawken (1993) offers several examples of appropriate green fees, including taxes on sewage effluent and airport landings. He devotes attention to the problems posed by hydrocarbons. Heavy reliance on petrochemicals and hydrocarbons—without full-cost accounting for their scarcity and the damage they do—is a major source of both economic inefficiency and environmental damage. He would remedy these problems with a substantial carbon tax based on the relative amounts of carbon in particular fuels.

To make his proposal politically achievable, Hawken (1993) would design these taxes both to be revenue neutral and so as not to effect any change in the net tax burden of different groups in society. For example, total revenue gains from a carbon tax would be offset with proportionate reductions in social security and income taxes. Thus the sum total of all taxes paid by the typical citizen of any income class would not change. Because low-income citizens spend a proportionately larger amount of their income on energy related products they would receive the largest percentage reductions in social security and income taxes. The possible regressivity of any tax is a familiar objection to green fees. Though Hawken (1993) appears unwilling to use the tax system to effect more equality in income distribution, he strives to ensure that energy taxation will not make that system any more regressive than it is. Unfortunately, he does not specifically discuss how to handle citizens who are on pensions or unemployment compensation, but presumably they too could be given direct compensation in the form of a "negative income tax" for increased energy costs. Americans with typical consumption patterns would find their total tax burden unchanged, but would have considerable economic incentives to change their purchases and lifestyles.

Hawken sees his agenda as one that will foster not only ecological integrity and efficiency but social justice as well. It will do so in three related ways: It will create new jobs, it will foster more localized economies, and it will encourage small business.

Hawken (1993) suggests that unemployment today is deeply embedded in the corporate effort to become more competitive and efficient through downsizing. He argues, however,

if sufficient incentives were in place, we might instead be focusing on quadrupling energy efficiency, realizing four times as much work from every kilowatt and calorie . . . This would not only solve our CO2 problem, but would also call for a massive increase in research, development, capital formation, jobs, and economic growth. It would benefit Northern and Southern nations alike, greatly reducing the amount of money spent in poorer countries on energy, and freeing them to be devoted to critical issues like food, water, health, and infrastructure. (p. 178)

Because such an approach would take away the artificial subsidies to carbon-fueled transit by taxing fossil fuels to reflect their true cost, it would encourage localities to rely more on local inputs. Local businesses could establish relationships of supply and interchange with other local firms, thereby providing a form of bootstrap economic development. Finally, in an economy that is relatively localized, small business would have more opportunity to survive and prosper. The relations between worker and employer in small business, Hawken (1993) believes, are often more egalitarian and more humane than in the large corporation. Social justice would also thrive.

Hawken's (1993) program is an admirable response to and provides direction for NIMBY politics, widespread concerns about social justice, and widely perceived deficiencies with governmental initiatives. The federal role is limited primarily to tax policy and to setting a few general standards regarding packaging and resource use. Popular concerns about harmful toxics, greenhouse gases, and depletion of scarce resources are all addressed.

Hawken's program is a decided improvement over more superficial corporate environmental efforts. Like the corporate initiatives, it seeks to build incentives into corporate life rather than to micromanage technologies from the outside. The Hawken program, however, strives for more than point of production pollution reduction. His taxes, which reflect relative resource scarcities and the damage technologies inflict across the full ecological spectrum, are far higher than any of the pollution taxes proposed by corporate environmentalists. There is an important reason for this. High levels of taxation are intended to effect new technologies and products that reduce pollution and conserve scarce resources throughout the whole product life-cycle. These offer the possibility of long-term ecological benefit and economic efficiency.

Nevertheless, there are reasons to doubt that Hawken's (1993) program would be as successful as he supposes. Even if his taxation policies—and therefore price changes—could be adopted, they would probably not by themselves foster the economic security needed to build the political support for a smooth transition to the ecologically sound economy he advocates. He would not pump any more federal money into the economy. His primary macroeconomic strategy is to increase green taxes dramatically while cutting other taxes. Hawken premises most of his faith in job creation on the notion that changing the target of taxation will foster a transformation from capital-intensive to labor-intensive industry and that such a change will create jobs. For example, Hawken relies on the familiar argument that solar power creates more jobs than nuclear power.

We wonder how much of a change in basic technology choices can be effected simply through tax policy. Large corporations have a major stake in existing technologies and may be able to resist moves to newly designed products and technology even as the price of their ecologically unsound inputs grows. We discuss this point further later in connection with Barry Commoner (1990). More fundamentally, small and labor-intensive firms would not necessarily dominate Hawken's economy. Nor should we necessarily be pleased if that were the result. Labor-intensive firms can often be low tech, low productivity, low wage, and insecure.

Hawken's emphasis on market mechanisms gives him an entree to popular media discussions of economics and ecology. It also gives him a kind of political plausibility we believe to be illusory. As the full scope of what Hawken (1993) intends becomes understood, his tax policy appears to be similar in important respects to the kinds of centralized command-and-control regulations he is trying to get beyond. Instead of micromanaging problems such as point of production toxics, he is trying to enact vast changes in the entire industrial infrastructure. That infrastructure is one in which U.S. firms have invested enormous capital and marketing commitment. For these reasons, his program, however purportedly market friendly, may appear more threatening to many powerful players than the much-lamented command-and-control approach.

That Hawken is using the language of the market is likely to be lost in the extreme constraints he is putting on the market. Worse, tax policy that would generate the degree of ecological benefits he seeks would itself be based on projections about resource use and depletion that will undoubtedly be controversial or subject to caricature—especially in periods of economic disruption. Because he does not explore the power relations extant in our primary corporate markets as they now exist, his proposals would be in for much rougher sledding than he indicates.

Hawken's (1993) assumptions in connection with equality, workplace organization, and growth are even more problematic. He seems to believe he solves these problems with his prescription for a much more localized economy, less dominated by the large corporation. He assumes that smaller corporations establish a more fair and egalitarian relationship with their workers. Like the Populists, he neglects the often inegalitarian origins and results of the market economy as it has evolved. Even if we could assume that his sustainability program could dramatically reverse a century of corporate concentration, will local businesses be so small as to lack substantial economic and political power?

Small is a relative term, of course. Classical economists investigate the processes through which small firms within genuinely free markets sort themselves out so that some achieve substantial power. Even in small communities, some firms gain prestige and easier access to local bank credit and attract the best workers. They then often achieve economies of scale and economic power by which they dominate those markets, rendering them less free. In addition, one might worry about the ability of successful firms to gain advantages through preferential access to local governments.

Ecologically, if markets were so insular and firms so small that economies of scale could not be achieved, misuse and overuse of resources might be more rampant. In any case, economically there would still be a tendency toward certain firms gaining leverage and, especially within Hawken's (1993) ideal of environmentally sound and genuinely competitive markets, such dominance might actually also be a consequence of good performance.

Even in the small-scale economy that Hawken pictures, some businesses will clearly be much more successful than others—both for good and bad reasons. These firms will likely be incorporated, have stockholders outside the immediate community, and try to amass substantial profits, especially in a competitive environment. One then can expect classic problems to emerge: oversaving by the wealthy as their incomes exceed their desire to spend, along with maximum automation of the workplace, lessening income and consumer demand. Total consumption may not be enough to sustain full employment, creating worker insecurity and augmenting the strength these firms have in their contact with workers with jobs. Unemployment and depressed salaries reestablish inequality.

Inequalities among regions could be an even greater risk than internal stratification. If economies do become genuinely local, they will reap the benefits or suffer the consequences of differential natural, capital, and human resource availability. Because communities, however defined, border on each other, such regional inequalities will be obvious. Weaker regions will be dominated by stronger ones, whose position is protected by the Constitution's establishment of a national free trade zone. These trends will aggravate interregional political problems.

Not all sustainability writers have been as optimistic on the subject of inequality as Hawken (1993) is. Herman Daly and John Cobb (1989) provide broad theoretical inspiration for such popular works as Hawken's. Yet Daly and Cobb more clearly acknowledge the reality of inequality in a market society and are willing to countenance redistributive taxation as a remedy. Free market advocates, however, often correctly argue that income redistribution can undermine motivation, whether of workers or of managers. If such subsidies are in direct proportion to the degree to which jobs are less well compensated and more menial, one can see why productivity could be harmed. Unless the intrinsic value of work increases, for many people the major incentive to work hard is the hope of moving up the ladder or accumulating enough to escape. Once those incentives are diminished, won't productivity problems exist in these jobs? Powerful economic constraints against provision of such subsidies are structured into our economy.

Social theorists and activists could devise policies to redistribute material resources in a way attuned to concerns for workplace productivity. These would, however, have to address issues beyond those in either Hawken's (1993) or Daly and Cobb's (1989) accounts. It would be necessary to examine work life and the ends that productivity serves. Such an analysis would include the questions of control in the workplace, the ways in which such control has shaped the needs and anxieties of workers, and how decisions about the use of future productivity gains are made. Indeed, failure to look at the relationship between incentives, work life, and consumer priorities blinds us as to why a range of income support programs become taboo subjects in contemporary political discourse. In addition, without addressing the anxieties created by work life and the priorities of growth itself, redistributive approaches to inequality will have little effect on what Juliet Schor (1991) calls the compulsion to shop and spend—and thereby go into debt. That addiction can be both a proximate cause of ineffective use of those funds people have and an environmental harm. Thus, even if we supplement Hawken's green market environmentalism with redistributive programs such as Daly and Cobb's, we are still likely to encounter serious economic and ecological problems, even as we find implacable political resistance to them.

Hawken (1993), like Daly and Cobb (1989), is trying to reconcile economic growth with environmental sustainability. Their reforms, if adopted, would do much good. The political sustainability of these programs, especially Hawken's, is suspect, however. His ideas, whatever their ecological merit, are likely to be lost in his program of massive—though revenue neutral—taxes and what amounts to forced reindustrialization.

One can imagine powerful constituencies not only of producers but also of workers coalescing early on to oppose Hawken's ecological agenda, especially because it makes no direct or obvious effort to address the insecurities of many citizens. Such opposition would focus on his grandiose tax policy, leaving the environment vulnerable to the long-term problems his tax policy is designed to solve.

Hawken's (1993) proposals presume both a level of economic effectiveness and a potential for political support, and therefore of environmental defense, that is not as self-evident as he suggests. Yet they remain politically attractive in one major respect: They begin within market culture and try to show us why we *must* and how we *can* really pay for what we buy or how we can decide to buy cheaper things because they are better. His argument, however, is predicated entirely on his belief that such a shift can be accomplished politically by its affinity for what he presumes to be contemporary political culture and the confidence that incentive-based systems deliver. In this, he misses the fact his environmental program also would face the same kinds of structural constraints and cultural binds that greet regulatory efforts.

An environmentally sound restructuring of the economy is inconceivable without substantial changes in job patterns by industry and region. Hawken (1993) assumes, as do corporate environmentalists, that markets will work this out in an equitable and efficient fashion once the green taxes are in place. Even if energy efficiency were to produce more jobs than nuclear power facilities,[1] such changes say nothing about who gets the jobs, their quality, or where they will be located.

Policies that implement new transit systems or solar collectors may be more ecologically and economically efficient in the long run but will be undermined unless we can keep a popular commitment to these options in place. These new technologies have major start-up costs. Society will be far more inclined to continue deferring its debt to nature unless the majority of citizens are assured they will not be unfairly and excessively burdened by this agenda. Nor does Hawken's program directly or convincingly address issues of distributive justice or ensure that the unused resources of this society—people whose skills and potential are not being fully used, including but not exclusively the unemployed[2]—can be used to foster these long-term gains. Only a program that achieves its efficiency by adequately and fairly employing all our citizens can sustantially reduce the burdens of ecological transition. These political and ethical requirements are magnified when we recognize that an industrial restructuring program of Hawken's sort will inevitably face even more substantial opposition than command-and-control programs ever did.

This resistance points us back to a comprehensive understanding of the weaknesses in Hawken's plan. It gives little sense as to why—except for the very important reason of enlightened environmental consciousness—people would make the transition away from present modes of production or how they would be able to free themselves from present needs and structures of power to do so.

Social Democratic Environmentalism

Consider now the work of the pioneer in the field of ecology and sustainable economics, Barry Commoner (1990). Hawken (1993), as well as many other environmentalists, draws creatively on Commoner's path-breaking work while compressing his agenda of reform. Like Hawken, Commoner proceeds from a reading of the failure of regulation to deal with the causes of environmental problems. Regulation is inadequate environmentally because it assumes that one can correct for the effects of faulty technology choices. He compares the few areas of regulatory success, in lead and mercury emissions, with those of failure, SO^2 and CO^2 emissions. The regulations were successful because government sought to prevent production in the first place. The failed regulations were unsuccessful because government allowed production and then sought to mitigate the consequences. The case of lead best illustrates the instinct the regulatory approach obeys. Government initially sought to regulate lead. Then, when research indicated that lead ruined the catalytic converters being developed to reduce automobile-produced smog, the government had no choice but to eliminate lead from fuel. Catalytic converters, designed to control rather than eliminate other pollutants, were essential to preserving the industry that produced gasoline-powered autos (Commoner, 1990, chap. 3).

Szasz's (1994) examination of the hazardous waste issues confirms Commoner's (1990) fear of industry power over regulation. Szasz reports that Congress was unable to rule out production of certain forms of hazardous and nonhazardous waste because of overwhelming business opposition to interference with technology choice. Instead, Congress settled on a complex set of standards as to safe levels of toxicity and how to achieve them through point of production control and disposal techniques for their byproducts. In trying to reconcile health with existing production and technology choices, the regulatory process thus finds itself in a dilemma. One could have environmentally ineffective but economically efficient standards or environmentally effective rules subject to the charge that they interfere with economic productivity. In a contest structured in this way, the environment usually loses.

Commoner (1990) argues that a successful marriage of economics and ecology is possible, but it must wed technologies to the demands of the ecological order from the ground up. Because humans occupy places in both an ecological and an economic order, if our actions in one realm produce problems in the other, damage eventually returns to the realm where it originated. Damage control is likely to be ineffective. The good news in Commoner's story is that there are modes of production and products that both reflect ecological needs and manage to be more profitable in the not-too-long run. For example, transit or energy utilities powered by alternative fuels could be made not only cost competitive but economically cheaper within a period of a few years. The ecological and economic orders can be reconciled. By Commoner's reckoning, this task can be achieved within the time frame of ecological tolerances, measured in terms of resource depletion and environmental damage, and depreciation schedules of, for example, utility generators, automobiles, and water heaters.

Commoner's work invites two immediate responses: This is too good to be true, and if these changes are so economically attractive as well as ecologically sound, why doesn't the private market make them? If ecologists are so smart, why aren't they rich? We address the first point fully later in this chapter. As for the second point, Commoner (1990) argues that large firms have made major investments in current technologies, they can make larger short-term profits by sticking to these technologies, and some industries that currently enjoy large profits would find their position prematurely threatened by moves of the sort he is discussing. Consistent with his line of analysis, Commoner could also argue that in an era when management operates under constraints posed by mutual and pension fund managers looking to achieve year-end profits rather than long-run gains, the time horizons of many American corporations have become extremely short. As Harvard economist William Lazonick (1992) points out, corporate management has itself become a marketable commodity and managers have become more wedded to the short-term bottom line than ever before.

New firms wishing to enter a field with environmentally sound technologies face daunting challenges—even if these technologies are economically viable. In mature industries, one cannot count on breaking in by creating demand for a new product. In cases where sounder technology has only a small cost advantage, even if one could get this news out, it is hard to lure customers away from old products and technologies. Some green products may require consumers to develop new habits. Yet supporting educational and service institutions and infrastructures are not in place to aid the transition to new products, new consumer choices, and new habits (Goodstein, 1995). When the start-up costs for new companies are considered, one can see a variety of barriers to entry new products must face.

The power that advertising often gives to established products further restricts the ability to compete. Attempts by environmental groups to stress the ecological advantages of cloth diapers have been met by a massive advertising defense of disposable diapers by consumer giant Proctor and Gamble. Defenders of the thesis that if alternative technologies were both economic and ecological, markets would have produced them, fail to reckon with the ways in which markets can concentrate power and the powerful can be expected to protect their positions. Markets are not just a sum total of equal private actors making rational choices.

Commoner (1990) believes that a major reason Americans have been unable to achieve a successful marriage of ecology and economics is the social belief that technology choices should be made by the private firm rather than by public authority. He is convinced that because these technologies threaten the conditions of our existence, we must exorcise this taboo. He argues for social intervention in technology choices. In particular, he would use tax policy to stimulate a move away from forms of energy, transit, and environmentally unsound petrochemical products. His proposal foreshadows that of Hawken (1993).

More ambitiously, however, Commoner (1990) would try to speed change through the use of government purchase policies to encourage economies of scale in the production of alternative products. Initial economies of scale would make these products more affordable and desirable to private consumers, fostering further economies and better competitive positioning. For industries—such as petrochemicals—that would be unable to fund their transition within the time frame imposed by the ecological danger they pose, he endorses direct federal subsidies.

Although he believes tax policy is important, Commoner believes Americans must do more because the market privileges corporate priorities in a way underappreciated by Hawken. Commoner draws political as well as economic lessons from this fact. We must build a broad coalition to overcome corporate resistance; Commoner understands that direct job creation is crucial to its construction. Social intervention is necessary for political as well as economic reasons. It makes such transitions more palatable to some extremely powerful economic actors. It also guarantees job security and creation in the period of transition, rather than simply holding out the theoretical idea that sustainable economic practices will produce jobs. It creates an economic underpinning for the kind of political coalition necessary for the changes Commoner seeks and disrupts the formation of those sure to oppose proposals such as those of Hawken.

Commoner in effect argues that, in an era in which current corporate priorities have entrenched advantages and social resources are underused, government spending, even deficit spending,[3] for long-term investments in ecological technologies, makes sense. It speeds an ecological transition in ways that allow the poor and the marginally employed to become a productive and esteemed part of society and thus eases the political burden in any economic transition.

Hawken's (1993) work is bold, insightful, and useful. Nevertheless, we regard Commoner (1990) as the better analyst. In particular, Commoner makes the more convincing argument as to the ways corporate power shapes technology choice. Because his diagnosis is more acute, his policy agenda offers more effective tools for achieving major technology change within a reasonable time frame. Nonetheless, Commoner, Hawken, and all advocates of a political economy that is ecologically sustainable must ask themselves why this kind of ecologically sound employment agenda has not gained more political presence than it has in an era of widespread concern about the environment.

We began to answer this question with our critique of Hawken's (1993) analysis, but now we need to interrogate Commoner's (1990) analysis as well. Commoner's reforms are geared primarily to achieve environmental benefits by mitigating, through government, the power imbalances between traditional and sustainable firms and, through democratic political intervention, between firms and enlightened consumers. There are two reasons to propel our analysis further into the limits both of political economy and of the major sustainability discourses. First, we need a more complete understanding of the constraints on sustainability agendas, including the reasons why people adopt ambivalent attitudes toward environmental reform. On the one hand, citizens believe in environmental values. On the other hand, aspects of the identities they form help reproduce the environmental problems. We suggest more is going on here than human reluctance to sacrifice for generally regarded goals. Second, if nature and human nature are less holistic and more unpredictable than environmentalists commonly assume, then respect for such uncertainties needs to be drawn into analytical framework and policy prescriptions. Both of these considerations suggest the need to affirm within sustainability discourse the importance of democratic politics within the realms of work life, culture, community, nation, and world. We now take up each of these points in turn.

The Limits of Social Democratic Ecology

Commoner (1990) pins much of his hope for reform on government investment in ecologically sound technologies and in the job production the development of these would entail. Indeed, new technological developments would have an immediate job creation effect and perhaps even some long-term gains through lowering the U.S. cost of production relative to world markets.

A certain degree of unemployment and poverty appears to be a necessary adjunct to the profitability of firms as they are currently structured in the U.S. political economy. Their profits and power also seem to be abetted, whether intentionally or not, by racial, ethnic, and gender injustices. A major reason for the failure of government spending to foster long-term full employment lies in the form management power takes in the contemporary workplace. The large corporation has been able to use its relative market position to charge higher prices and, during flush eras, to pay somewhat higher wages. For this wage premium it has exacted a charge in the form of routinized and highly supervised jobs.

Many economists have long suggested that such jobs are simply a consequence of technology development and therefore are the price we pay for greater social affluence. Yet there is considerable reason to believe that the structure of work life in modern economies has not followed some invariant, technological imperative. Comparable industrially advanced factories do not all have the same work life structures. For example, some Western European, some Japanese, and even a few U.S. factories have allowed workers at least some input into the design of the job process itself (Buell, 1995, chap. 2; Tyson & Levine, 1990).

In the U.S. case, elaborate job hierarchies disorganize employees, pitting them against one another in individual quests for management's favor. These techniques, when uncontested, lessen workers' ability to win wage or work life concessions within the firm or to join fights for broader full employment outside it. Racial, ethnic, and gender tensions—whether fueled by management or not—have sometimes further aggravated divisions within the workplace. However much these workplaces may succeed in buttressing management power, they are far from models of efficiency. Supervision, or indirect labor, is a high cost of production in the modern U.S. firm. In addition, workers who have little input into or knowledge of the production process cannot rapidly retool that process or aid in the innovation of products.

A number of studies have shown that where workers have more substantial input and knowledge and share in the profits, productivity increases far more rapidly (Bluestone & Bluestone, 1993; Buell, 1995). In addition, more democracy within the production process seems to mean a more egalitarian distribution of income. There is not as great a disparity in skills, and workers are in a better bargaining position.

A number of factors within our economy militate against such productivity and equity gains, however. Workers in whom management has vested neither substantial education nor responsibilities are easier to replace and control. They are poorly positioned to know about or to limit employer efforts to move plants or pursue mergers or other means of boosting short-term profits to the detriment of long-term economic and environmental advance. Most U.S. managers have thus far resisted efforts to give workers more than token voices in their own jobs.

When an economy organized along conventional lines does grow and produce high levels of employment, workers are also in a better position to voice discontent, either by organizing unions or by quitting and moving on. As employment tightens, firms both experience and anticipate profit squeezes from worker militancy. The lesson management learns from this is that some degree of unemployment is necessary to secure control over the work process. This lesson is implemented at both the level of the firm and the overall economy. Although management could democratize workplaces and agree with workers to convert sales growth into shared investments in new plants and a redesigned workplace, instead they reduce investment in new plants. They also lobby the government for policy that reduces the demand for workers: cuts in federal spending and increases in interest rates. Joblessness increases, as does talk about the natural rate of unemployment. The rate is natural for those who assume no viable alternatives exist to current workplace structures.

A sustainability agenda that creates full employment therefore will also have to be strong enough to create support for reform of work life. Such strength is dependent on healing existing breaches within the constituencies that would benefit the most from such reforms, even as the reforms are needed to overcome the divisions.

The politics of class and the politics of "identity" around race, gender, and ethnicity cannot be neatly dissociated, as we will discuss further in subsequent chapters. In U.S. culture, identity formation may sometimes have involved a process of easing inner doubts about one's own values, associates, or life projects by conceiving those who differ along any of these lines as inferior. Thus a white male blue- or white-collar worker may resent black welfare recipients for a constellation of reasons. He may harbor historic racial attitudes, which may themselves in part be constructed from and intensified by doubts about disciplines he swallows or even imposes on himself. He may project onto others his own desire to escape these disciplines—and then repress this desire by condemning as innately inferior those who do seem to him to evade some of the disciplines of modern industrial and postindustrial life. (Campbell, 1992; Clarke 1993; DeLuca, 1995 chap. 12)

Such resentments also exist in a specific historical setting. It is clear to some that African Americans, for example, have gained legal equality and even affirmative help. What remains obscure, and far less discussed in major cultural media, is that educational disadvantages, poorer job prospects, and an array of unintended and explicit practices of exclusion, from redlining regarding housing loans to pervasive school segregation to seniority work rules, have limited these gains. Especially in a cultural context of increased belief in laissez-faire economics and meritocracy, these disadvantages may appear as displaying inferiority and attempts to remedy them may appear as special pleading. When tax, welfare, and job creation policies either ask or can easily be portrayed as asking white workers to pay much of the cost of social justice programs, resentments toward caricatured targets become rigidified. In the absence of a more synthetic democratic program, when explicit efforts are made to address the effects of present and past racial exclusion, these social programs sometimes have had the unfortunate and unintended effect of further reinforcing racial antagonisms.

Why doesn't an agenda of full employment through environmental job creation automatically win full support from all citizens? The beginning of an answer lies in the possibility that some citizens may interpret universal programs as veiled efforts to help suspect groups. The political consequences are palpable in a postindustrializing economy in which gaps in wealth are widening. As Thomas and Mary Edsall (Edsall & Edsall, 1991) argue,

> In spite of American success in eliminating legally protected racial subjugation, race remains a powerful wedge issue, and as long as that is the case, the incentive to capitalize on racial conflict will supersede pressures to address the economic bifurcation that increasingly plagues the country. (p. 284)

Whites may not be alone in blocking the development of broad coalitions. Minorities may fear that they will get at best the crumbs from such programs and insist instead on affirmative programs that exclusively help people like themselves. The history of other welfare state policies on full employment is instructive in this regard. New Deal job creation focused primarily on construction jobs, which went almost exclusively to males. The urban liberalism of the Fair Deal increased employment opportunities for some African Americans, but left them far behind most whites in income and job opportunities. Many of the centerpiece urban projects of the 1950s and 1960s displaced poorer African Americans from their homes (Clarke, 1993). Even programs addressed specifically to minorities' needs, such as elements of the war on poverty and affirmative action, either have been abandoned or are under assault.

Environmental regulation itself is a program thought to be universal, but its current application also undermines support for a sustainability program by placing unfair burdens both on working-class and nonwhite communities. For example, corporate and governmental authorities often displace the costs of environmental regulation from more affluent to poorer communities by designating them as toxic disposal sites. As Robert Bullard (1993) shows, there is also a direct connection between race and injustice in environmental programs. Class factors alone are an insufficient indicator of where dumps have gone or will go. Even when income is controlled for, dumps are more likely to be placed in minority communities.

How does one explain these trends? These communities are vulnerable not simply because they have faced more obstacles to organizing politically but also because of the attitudes of the white majority toward their plight. With many whites believing minorities already receive special treatment, minority protest that their neighborhoods be spared are often met with indifference, if not annoyance.

If toxic production were limited, less would go into minority—and working-class white—neighborhoods, and increased demand for new production technologies might create some jobs for these communities. Nonetheless, inequities regarding race, gender, and ethnicity lodged within business and union practices will not necessarily be eliminated by broader employment, nor will the division of labor that continues within the household. Without explicit efforts to explore the deeper personal and cultural underpinnings of such patterns of exclusivity, broad support for a full employment ecology program is easily undermined. We cannot simply wish the social issues away. At least as far back as Populism, conservatives have been able to drive a spike though the heart of reform by denigrating the character of suspect groups whom universal programs will or are helping. One can, for instance, imagine attacks on an ecological full employment program based on criticism of the "inexperienced and irresponsible" citizens being hired for that program. These characterizations would be code words for race. Even an environmental agenda is not immune to the ghost of Willie Horton. Improving the number and quality of jobs creates the best context for moving beyond the politics of exclusion, but is no substitute for direct consideration of it.

Commoner (1990) is very sensitive to and concerned about issues of race and gender. Indeed, he is a pioneer in trying to demonstrate the relationship between issues that, within popular political discourse, often seem separate. His concern is also more than academic. He has spent much of his life in the political pursuit of a more just society. He has been a civil rights advocate, a presidential candidate, and a major supporter of and adviser to Jesse Jackson. Clearly he supports not only maximum civil rights enforcement but also strong positive measures to redress past disadvantages and believes these are a necessary constituent of any environmental program. He articulates his concerns well when he argues that there is "an unbreakable link between the environmental issue and all the other troublesome political issues . . . environmentalism reaches a common ground with all the other movements" (quoted in Szasz, 1994, p. 153).

By underspecifying the connections between an environmental full employment program and race and gender justice, workplace organization, and certain identities spawned in the larger political culture, however, Commoner's (1990) analysis leaves gaps that need filling. Will environmentally sound technologies necessarily resolve issues of social cost displacement, especially differential treatment based on race, class, and gender? Would the jobs these technologies create alter the organization of the workplace? If Commoner's reforms are not more explicitly focused in these areas, will the kinds of coalitions needed to support his agenda be feasible?

These problems are especially important for us to consider today because, unlike Commoner (1990), many contemporary commentators reject the significance of difference. The idea that socioeconomic class transcends race for all intents and purposes is popular across the political spectrum. Most often this view is predicated on the corollary belief that once class is transcended, so too will difference be. In classic free market theories, discrimination is inefficient, costly, and irrational. Competition dissolves these anachronisms by driving out of business firms that practice them. Neoconservatives and New Democrats argue that, with the adoption and enforcement of equal opportunity laws, racial and ethnic differences primarily become cultural differences and a vestige of the past. If minorities would change their values to those of the opportunity society, they too would succeed. Among some Leftists, racial, ethnic, and gender divisions are epiphenomena of class society, useful for aiding the process of labor market segmentation. Once capitalism has been either transcended or radically reformed, such differences will fade.

In pure form, each of these orientations is insensitive to both the historic and the contemporary independence of inequity rooted in perceived physical differences. There is a danger of lapsing into a kind of racism or sexism to the degree that difference is not more carefully assessed and addressed. Although none of the proponents of these theories would intentionally naturalize gender or racial differences, silence can easily restore the role of nature in grounding difference, thereby supporting patterns of inferiority and superiority. Why do certain kinds of people have the attitudes they hold, and why are others in positions to be exploited?

In contemporary capitalism, as well as throughout the history of socialism, significant general differences in wealth and income for women and minorities persist.[4] Observing persisting inequalities by race under modern capitalism, some conservatives fall back on the assertion that those who do not make it are inferior in terms of inner capacity (Hernstein & Murray, 1994; *New Republic*, 1994). More responsible conservatives attribute the failure to a persistent unwillingness of certain groups to internalize appropriate values, too often leaving unanswered the question why specific subordinate groups internalize values different from those of dominant groups. Even this explanation seems to place the onus of failure on the "natural makeup" of the group in question and runs the risk of becoming a veiled form of racism (Clarke, 1993; Winant, 1994). Denying the effect that different starting points and life chances have on development and failing to scrutinize the concepts employed in assessing intelligence puts certain racial groups at a disadvantage.

Modern socialist and social democratic states have seen the continuity of severe race and gender inequities. Some radicals characteristically respond to these widely recognized inadequacies by suggesting that no one ever fully tried socialism; if they had, the remaining racial or gender inequalities would no longer persist. Such remarks are reminiscent of Bertrand Russell's famous line about Christianity to the effect that it would be a great religion if anyone ever tried it. This analysis begs a question: Why is it so hard to get the population to embrace socialist or capitalist universalism if race and gender are merely epiphenomena?

How one understands the boundaries of race groups varies historically. Some on the Left hold onto their model of economic development or economic progress as a kind of identity marker almost as tightly as some premodern groups held onto their forms of racial or tribal identification. Without substantial movement toward greater economic equality and independence, citizens are unlikely to shake exclusive forms of identity. Nonetheless, without more self-conscious recognition of the reasons for exclusive forms of identity, reductionist politics, and even economic reductionism, we may be blinded to some of the real causes of the injustices that we must overcome to enable less dogmatic forms of identity to emerge.

Speaking at the level of immediate policy, a full employment ecology program would not guarantee equally fulfilling and challenging jobs to minorities and women. Nor would it automatically provide adequate environments for all families and their children. Many families today are headed by single women with inadequate child support. Too many such families are poor—a phenomenon known as the *feminization of poverty*. Just as with other low-income groups, these poor, female-headed households face inordinate risks of environmental exposure, though we are not familiar with any current study of environmental sexism connected with the effects of waste disposal placement or related issues.

Better job opportunities would help poor women, but even here a word of caution is needed. A large portion of the jobs in social democratic ecology programs would involve factory construction—new modes of energy or transit, as well as massive retrofitting of insulation and solar or alternative heating systems. An increased commitment to these areas, necessary as it is, will have the immediate effect of providing jobs disproportionately for men—given prevalent opportunity structures and hiring patterns. This would have to change. An adequate full employment program would also have to ask what kinds of economic opportunities are being created for teachers, public health nurses, and other service providers, roles in which women today actually find many employment chances—however much these gender roles, too, have to change. Jobs in these areas have implications not only for social justice but for ecology as well, and need to be emphasized in a democratic ecology program.

In addition, we should examine the area of occupational safety with particular focus on gender. To the extent that corporate or government policy denies women access to jobs that might pose a disproportionate risk to their reproductive health, it also limits important opportunities. Clearly, for corporations and governments to allow women to compete as equals, there is a case here for making the workplace safe for all.

Another major gap in the social democratic ecology program lies in its commitment to growth in goods and services as the prime vehicle through which to redress inequalities of any sort. Unreflective commitment to growth, even less resource-intensive modes, reinforces those bases of respect within identities of working people that depend on shop and spend. In the process, it often fosters the need to disparage alternative sets of values—not only among others but even within one's own life. We must address the ways in which workplace organization, acquisitive individualism, and mass culture undermine opportunities for broader forms of individuality and cultural difference. Indeed, these may require too much focus on consumption. The need to have and own more may in turn impose a host of resource and environmental constraints and interdependencies requiring ever more social and personal discipline. In such a context, dogmatic identities gain greater purchase even as many of us quietly chafe under their disciplines or surreptitiously (deceiving even ourselves sometimes) evade them.

Commoner (1990) has been a leader in suggesting that an adequate ecological agenda is more than a technical problem. The command-and-control agenda of earlier liberals failed because its complexity, its limited results, and the economic burdens with which it was associated allowed corporate groups to mobilize a majority against its means, if not its aims. But if regulatory efforts fail in part because of lack of support, to what degree can we expect prevention programs to gain the support to replace them?

Commoner's (1990) program could achieve more gains on the ecological front and surely more job creation than either corporate environmentalism or Hawken's (1993) ecopopulism. Commoner is correct to argue that prevention programs have the potential to build an important support constituency. We argue, however, that an ecological program with full employment can be sustained only through the vehicle of a democratic politics that more fully considers contemporary identity formation.

Growth, Nature, and the Workplace

Commoner (1990) is eloquent on the idea that if the United States adopts the right policies, nature can become a home and resource for Americans:

Certain molecular arrangements are shunned in the chemistry of life. Thus, very few chlorinated organic compounds . . . occur in living things. This suggests that the vast number of such compounds that are possible chemically . . . have been rejected in the long course of evolution as biological components. The absence of a particular substance from nature is often a sign that it is incompatible with the chemistry of life. "Nature knows best" is shorthand for the view that during the several billion years in which they have evolved, living things have created a limited but self-consistent array of substances and reactions that are essential to life. (pp. 12-13)

Commoner reminds us that nature imposes limits on our technology, which we neglect at our peril. He has been a leader in bringing discussions in scientific ecology into the center of economic debate. Scientific ecology is, however, a field in flux. Many of its debates, although beyond the scope of this work, clearly have analogues with issues we are considering.

Commoner (1990) reminds us that the web of life is extraordinarily complex and our knowledge is always partial. He insufficiently develops a corollary to this, however. Many contemporary ecologists argue that non-human nature demonstrates boom and bust cycles of its own and that the process of evolution itself is neither smooth nor continuous. Thus, Martin O'Connor (1994a) remarks that human and natural systems are not only in a process of complex interaction with each other, but that the internal activity of each system is to some degree autonomous and thus by extension creates unpredictability for the other one. Not only may humans create ecological problems for nonhuman nature, but nonhuman nature is fully capable of doing the same for humans regardless of human behavior. This picture of nature is best expressed in Georges Canguilhem's classic *On the Normal and the Pathological* (1991). Canguilhem remarks, " For the living being, life is not a rectilinear movement, it ignores geometrical rigidity, it is a discussion . . . with an environment where there are leaks, holes, escapes, and unexpected resistances" (p. 198).

The implication of such a picture is that there are no completely predictable regularities or balances in nature on which material growth or complex and completely determinant patterns of interaction can be unproblematically constructed. Although no ecologist holds the absurd position that nature is utterly chaotic, many contemporary ecologists now question the utility or universal applicability of such notions as ecosystems.[5] Nature may surprise even the best sustainability agenda or may prove more resilient than proponents fear. This added sense of unpredictability remains a cautionary tale, requiring both anticipation of the possibility of disruption of essential resources and consideration of how the best technologies may themselves prove dangerous.

If the faith in nature as orderly balance or stable hierarchy is found wanting, another form of faith may be more appropriate. Many studies suggest that transformation of our technologies in the direction of solar power and alternatively fueled vehicles makes ecological sense with regard to such problems as greenhouse effect and the hole in the ozone layer. Just as important is the way such technologies could make us less dependent on complex, extensive, and fragile lines of supply. Nonetheless, we should not simply assume that such technologies will not have significant but unanticipated public health or ecological implications, even as we appreciate their superiority to conventional fossil and nuclear fueled technologies. Can we be sure about the ecological effects that may flow from placing solar reflectors on hundreds of millions of houses or dotting large areas of the countryside with windmills?

Commoner (1990) is right to point to the ways in which the unregulated quest for profits places ecologically unsound constraints on technology choices. Suppose that technology choices are made by an independent scientific agency established by an ecologically astute and concerned Congress. The most prudent production of technology and its monitoring, however, requires citizen and worker involvement at the point of production and in the community, something Commoner supports but doesn't build fully into his analysis. Even contemporary technologies are not shaped simply through top-down insight, but by the hands-on work of technicians.

It is at the point of production or in the community that problems with a technology often first become apparent—and to those most adversely affected. Granting these citizens a voice in development, implementation, and oversight makes technologies more comprehensible, enabling better oversight in the future. These opportunities help ensure support for sustainable technologies.

There are many ways that a distant public authority can make mistakes about technology choice, including excessive commitment to overall economic growth to the exclusion of concerns voiced by specific groups. Alternative social and economic criteria must be developed through forums that include worker and resident input. Such a process further enhances worker and citizen monitoring skills and the value of their contributions to protecting the larger regional or national community. For all its failings, U.S. environmental law's emphasis on citizen ability to comment on government regulatory and construction decisions, as well as on placement of some private factories and dumps, has made a substantial contribution to an informed and alert public. One only needs to compare the American decision process with that of the Soviets on nuclear power to see the importance of citizen involvement at the community level.

Workers are often the first to spot problems, and the workplace is often the first locus of industry-induced public health problems. Keeping workers from broad knowledge of the production process squanders an important safeguard. Even as alternative technologies are developed through tax and subsidy policies, worker and community knowledge remains crucial. Change will lag behind in some economic areas—perhaps a product of scientific and economic uncertainties and unpredictabilities—producing ecological "hot spots." Citizen and worker participation is critical to identifying these and remedying their effects.

If unpredictability is a hallmark of both ecological and human systems, one needs to design an economy keeping in mind the possibility of accident. This entails not only the establishment of some kinds of warning systems for centralized industrial failure but also care in the preservation of localized biological, food, and energy resources. These serve as ultimate fallbacks should patterns of technological interdependence break down. Such a vision should not entail the literal community self-sufficiency endorsed by some radical environmentalists, with all the inefficiencies, inequality, and even deprivations it would likely entail. It does require development patterns more dependent on the community and region, particularly regarding necessities. This approach provides insurance against unpredictable disasters as well as cost savings from reduced energy use.

Commoner (1990) emphasizes specific technologies as the key to the solution of ecological problems, but, as with Hawken (1993), a significant gap exists. Commoner, unlike many mainstream and radical environmentalists, correctly recognizes that growth in goods and services is more necessary for poorer nations and social classes. Nonetheless, he fails to ask why growth becomes more of an imperative than a choice for many middle-class citizens and whether economic growth as we presently construe it seems too often to lean against designing an environmentally sound economy. Even if growth were to continue along lines that did not stress scarce hydrocarbons or add to the greenhouse threat, might it not pose other ecological problems?

Here we return to some of the strengths in Polanyi's (1957) analysis. We have an economy in which substantial inequalities among citizens exist, in which work life is organized hierarchically and working hours are determined by the firm. Product priorities are left in private hands with limited information. In such an economy, individuals will continue to need ever more products to meet the social and practical needs created by the consumption of others, to get a good job, or even to hold onto certain prized social relations. Pursuit of growth unreflectively seems to produce a dialectic between control over nature and control over people that causes both ecological and social harm.

Consider again the ecological implications of the workplace. Many of the better craft jobs were "deskilled" during the late 19th and early 20th century era of corporate reorganization of the workplace. This deskilling process was further buttressed by the establishment of elaborate and highly artificial hierarchies among workers whose skill levels differed little. Such processes were designed not only for technological advancement but also to deprive workers of effective bargaining power within the firm. Jobs could be restructured to challenge and stimulate workers more. Such workers would be more productive, but they would also enjoy a better bargaining position. Thus far U.S. industry has not been interested in making that bargain.

With the rise of postindustrial technologies, a new premium has been placed on the high-technology or knowledge worker. Although a few highly educated technicians with considerable skills and opportunities do occupy key positions in many high-technology firms, U.S. industry has managed to structure the new work in ways that Frederick Taylor (discussed in Buell, 1995) would recognize. True, the modern worker on the electronic production line must have certain keyboarding and basic math and reading skills not possessed by an earlier generation. Nonetheless, much of the work is still largely rote and learned far more quickly than is usually acknowledged (Garson, 1988).

Despite all the talk about the need for educated workers, nearly one fifth of college-educated workers work at jobs for which their education is not relevant. Kathleen Newman and Chauncy Lennon (1995) report that, in New York City, many McDonald's restaurants now seek high school graduates. Burger flipping has not become more knowledge intensive.

In addition to maintaining elaborate and artificial job hierarchies, management often keeps hours long. Such a policy makes the loss of a job a major crisis and limits the number of workers who receive benefits. Using a core of long-hour workers also leaves a pool of unemployed or underemployed workers whose availability is a continual reminder that anyone can be replaced. Workers have two alternatives. They can strive to advance to the few jobs that offer an opportunity for self-respect and personal development. Or they can seek satisfaction and respect off the job. If time and opportunity for private leisure and public recreation diminish, consumption itself often becomes a mode of self-expression or a quick fix for temporarily escaping the tedium and stress of the job. One shows who one is by the clothes one wears, the restaurants one frequents, the camps one sends one's children to, the vacations one takes. The more exclusive the choices—that is, the harder for others to attain—the more suitability for advancement in the ranks. Meanwhile, as some luxuries become necessities, some citizens need to purchase more goods just to preserve access to traditional amenities.

In the process, a constituency for ecologically unsustainable economic growth is constructed. Firms must grow to survive. Because they eschew worker participation as a way to increase productivity, they closely regulate workers. Workers are constrained to accept these disciplines and seek rewards elsewhere. Businesses augment such growth by constantly expanding and marketing the product lines that people are encouraged to purchase, but for which they must work more to afford. Citizens are shooting at a moving target just as surely as they must not stop aiming at it.

As work life and commodities take up inordinate portions of life, opportunities for satisfaction outside this treadmill also recede. Perhaps this is one reason writers across the political spectrum define the treadmill of work and production as what life is really about. In a society where so many seek relief from stress, where time always seems to be an issue, one might ask why is there so little open political discussion of the need for growth of this scarce item.

There is increasing evidence that many today do find Americans' preoccupation with the cycle of work and spend unavoidable, unfulfilling, and ecologically threatening. The popular media, especially advertising, are full of discussions of the harried character of modern life. A recent advertisement for Delta Airlines delivers the stressed executive from a frantic day to a healthy, relaxing dive into a pool—which is shaped like a clock.

Polls reflect Delta's marketing choices. Although a majority of Americans would not wish to trade any of their present wages for cuts in hours worked, they would be willing to take future increases in productivity in the form of hour reductions rather than higher wages (Schor, 1991). Polls and ads are hardly conclusive, but they do call into question the easy assumptions about popular resistance to thinking more about qualitative advancement and less about gross measures of economic growth.

Until the late New Deal, a major goal of American unions was to achieve shorter working hours. The purposes were several, including job creation and hourly wage gains. Unions also were concerned with quality of life, including time for family and recreation. In the choice between the Wagner Labor Act, whose major provisions dealt with union rights to organize for higher wages, and the Black-Connery Act, which would have dramatically shortened working hours, corporate leadership lobbied Franklin Roosevelt to support the former. Interestingly enough, especially in light of today's antiunionism, many larger corporations in the 1930s were more accepting of unions than of government programs to shorten hours (Hunnicutt, 1988).

Corporations today are as united in opposition to hours reduction as ever. Are there any reasons beyond the narrowly economic ones we have already cited? To imply that growth is not an end in itself, or at least not the only one, as hours reduction would, suggests that compelling alternatives to consumerism exist. Such alternatives challenge especially the identities and status of managers, who today tie up entire lives in the firm and reap very large material rewards, rewards many view as proof of their virtue.

Questions such as these must be distinguished carefully from legitimate concerns about economic security and equity. Moreover, economic insecurity breeds environmental indifference and fuels unreflective commitment to further growth. Where poverty exists, where many people work long hours in insecure jobs, and where communities are continually vulnerable to capital flight, there will be pressures against taking interest in a range of long-term environmental amenities. By the same token, greater economic security and more time to enjoy the outdoors can lead to greater interest in environmental preservation. Cross-cultural scholarship suggests such a conclusion. In Sweden, citizens have enjoyed—at least until recently—fairly secure incomes and have been able to convert some of their productivity gains into shorter hours. In so-called contingent valuation studies they placed high value on open space and farmland. Their concerns extend not only to their desire to enjoy undeveloped land, but to pass it on to future generations (Vail, Hasund, & Drake, 1994).

Where does this analysis lead? However much we all share some nostalgia for a time that, perhaps, never existed, there is no turning back. Hawken (1993) wishes to get us back to the free market. But this free market brought us to where we are today. Polanyi (1957) recalls traditional societies, but their modes of social and economic development bred forms of discipline and oppression that have been obliterated in most of the world.

Many environmentalists celebrate the small community; indeed, there are good reasons to give communities more control over transit, energy, and economic policies. Solution of difficult problems requires levels of consensus that can emerge only through some kind of directly participatory politics. Nevertheless, the faith some radical environmentalists have in the "natural" size, shape, and content of businesses and communities needs to be challenged. Communities must reach out though a complex process of negotiating across borders; often, they must question the kind of consensus that emerges even internally. Large-scale enterprise—when properly conceived—can often deliver more to workers and citizens.

Neither the local community nor the self-sufficient household as solution to all problems or as source of all value can become a mantra for a successful program of sustainability. Communities—however defined—would pay a high price for giving each other complete control over a range of policy questions. Complete local control over transit, health, and environmental regulation would be purchased at best at the cost of an almost complete randomness of results, as each community's decisions impinge inevitably on the acts of others. At worst, it would trigger massive inequities and even conflicts as communities affected adversely by their neighbors respond in kind. Most likely, however, talk of the small community as the only proper source of decisions makes its proponents politically irrelevant. It weighs environmentalism down with utopian caricatures, and thus unwittingly contributes to a process of economic and political centralization that has already gone too far.

A new political interpretation is needed. We require a perspective that points to the ways work life, consumer, and corporate priorities could be reformed without fostering an omnipotent state or oppressive communities. It would work through markets as the best currently known method to foster decentralized coordination of economic decisions, but would understand that these too are tools in need of democratic intervention if they are to remain as free as possible.

This would celebrate individual initiative. Indeed, it would make it more possible for each person to determine his or her future. It would not rule out the need for more material growth—especially for the poorest, who still have obvious needs for adequate housing, transportation, and health care. It would, however, temper the contemporary growth imperative and make growth more a reflective choice, susceptible to debates about the ends to which it will be put. Finally, it would not be cost-free. A new form of social responsibility is necessary, replacing existing disciplines with others. It would ask us to meet the obligations necessary to sustain a decent life, in part by modulating some demands we make of each other and nature simply to confirm our present ways of being. In a world of change and interdependence, meeting this requirement will entail a challenge that only democratic politics could hope to negotiate fairly.

At the end of the day, this new orientation will still have to demonstrate that—all things being equal—it can generate a superior quality of life for ourselves and future generations. Because it opens up so much space for democratic politics, its value and importance will always be up for assessment. Perhaps that is one of its strengths.

We turn now to some of the broader philosophical considerations that inform this view and some of the policy agendas and debates that might emerge if this perspective were to gain a more substantial presence in our society.

Notes

1. This is a familiar argument against nuclear power, nuclear weapons, and other high-technology systems. It asserts that capital-intensive projects are not efficient job creators. Part of this argument, however, turns on the fact that nuclear power hires many relatively highly paid technicians. Surely a broad-based alternative program will also need to hire some well-schooled technical people. In any case, even if Hawken's (1993) implicit job program would create more jobs than we imagine, it still would run up against the kind of workplace problems we discuss in connection with Barry Commoner (1990).

2. Hawken (1993) does not provide a thorough examination of unemployment in this society, which is undercounted by official statistical categories. This is an important point. One way to defray the social cost of the transition to new and more efficient technologies is to make sure that citizens are able to get productive jobs. The theme of joblessness and job statistics is discussed in Buell (1995, chap. 4).

3. We cannot discuss here all the problems with the current obsession with balanced budgets. Suffice it to say that we believe it is appropriate for governments to borrow money for long-term capital improvements, just as it is for corporations. Deficit spending has gone awry because of imperfect modes of economic internationalization, because deficits have gone to the wrong targets, and because any full employment policy runs up against problems

in the contemporary workplace, as we discuss below. For more on this, see Buell (1995), chaps. 2 and 4.

4. On gender justice in socialism, see Scott (1974). The persistence of relatively low income and wealth among African Americans in this country is widely documented. For the effect of Reaganomics on women's situation, see Bowles, Gordon, and Weisskopf (1993). A major exception to these trends is Sweden, where women are nearly at income parity. Nonetheless, this case demonstrates our point because the women's movement in Sweden has raised these issues within the context of social democratic politics.

5. We are indebted for this analysis to Anderson (1995). Anderson recognizes temporary and shifting patterns on which species protection can be carried out, but is critical of homeostatic and totalizing equilibrium models. He is especially cogent in pointing to the limits of the concept of ecosystem itself.

4 Nature, Human Nature, and Community

Community and Ecology

The internalization of common values undergirds voluntary compliance with informal standards and laws governing behavior. Without shared norms of some sort, only the police can hold society together. Failure to recognize that market norms alone may be insufficient mars much corporate environmentalism.

Nonetheless, if common norms are in some sense necessary, as is argued by holistic environmentalists, they also succeed in part by exclusion. An ecological agenda thus ultimately will be sustainable only to the extent that it also valorizes democracy's role in guarding against the imperialism of community. Common purposes are never simple, fully shared, all-encompassing, or above debate, however necessary they may be to the community. Political and social interaction within and between levels of government and voluntary associations fashions community from unstable and recalcitrant human and nonhuman resources.

Some ecofundamentalist programs veer toward a form of moral imperialism. These theories begin with the recognition that the survival of the species requires coming together to some degree on certain goals and ends. They move to the more questionable assumption that one common agenda can fit each of us without remainder, to borrow a phrase from Bonnie Honig (1993).

Honig (1993) contrasts two perspectives on politics and democracy. *Virtue theorists* of politics assume that "the world and the self are not resistant to, but only enabled and completed by, their favored conceptions of order and subjectivity" (p. 3). *Virtù theorists* "argue that no such fit is possible" (p. 3). Because every social agenda leaves discrepancies in its wake, politics must be seen not as a transitory means to a final social harmony but as a continual process of lessening the burdens placed on the inevitable "remainders" of each new settlement. Though politics, from such a perspective, never ends and never gets it quite right, the political order that seeks continually to foster as much space as possible for difference will elicit more respect for law and greater political legitimacy.

Much of modern ecopopulist and ecofundamentalist discourse follows the virtue model. Low or appropriate technology is seen as fostering greater local self-sufficiency, more opportunity for face-to-face interactions, heightened awareness of humans' dependence on an interconnection with the natural world, and more of a commitment to small communities as themselves "natural." The dissonance, trade-offs, and dangers of such alleged harmonies are all shuffled out of this picture, as is politics itself—all on the wings of a largely unexamined teleology of nature.

Murray Bookchin (1985), whose philosophical works have influenced a range of popular thought on sustainable economics, expresses these sentiments in their most thoroughgoing and eloquent form:

> The only agent on which we can premise future radical change emerges from a melding of traditional groups into a public sphere, a body politic, a community imbued with a sense of cultural and spiritual continuity and renewal. This community, however, is constituted only in the ever present act of an ever-dynamic effort of public self-assertion that yields a sharp sense of self-hood. Collectivity thus merges with individuality to produce rounded human beings in a rounded society. Direct action assumes the form of direct democracy: the participatory forms of freedom that rest on face to face assemblies . . . and where possible, consensus. (p. 71)

Thus the small community offers not only ecological benefits but a form of sociality that threatens no aspect of individuality. The echoes of Rousseau (1762/1988) are very strong.

There are good reasons to reduce our dependence on distant resources and to seek greater community. Nonetheless, there is little besides a teleological faith in nature's providence to suggest that every small community can become completely self-sufficient or that every so-called natural technology is free from unanticipated effects on its own or surrounding communities.

Those of us who have lived or worked in small communities know that, for all their many strengths, they are always to some extent both intrusive and exclusionary. The very fact that the community is small, face to face, and participatory can lead many to assume—even when their own immediate needs are frustrated—that the community knows best.

As we think about such issues, it might be wise, as William Connolly (1992) suggests, to entertain the thought that perhaps nature—including human nature—was not designed as a safe home for us any more than it was designed as an endless resource for our economic purposes or a sink for their detritus. Human history shows us to be creatures who have constituted nature—and human nature—in different ways at different times. In our own existential insecurity, we often claim our values to be natural and therefore absolute. We use those claims to legitimize our favored forms of community.

Charles Taylor's (1985a) discussion of the human need for a grounding solidly in or above nature may be read as one of the most eloquent manifestations of what Connolly (1992) would label *ontological narcissism*:

> The analogy is that in both cases we have a place to stand outside the context of human emotions in order to determine what is truly important. In one case, that of tradition, this is seen as a larger order which is the locus of more than human significance. In the modern case, it is an order of nature which is meant to be understood free of any significance at all, merely naturalistically. And this is by no means a minor difference. That is not my claim. Rather it is that beyond this difference, something of the same aspiration is evident in both. And this is linked with my belief that the aspiration to spiritual freedom, to something more than the merely human, is much too fundamental a part of human life ever to be set aside. It goes on—only under different forms—and even under forms where it is essential that it does not appear as such. That is the paradox of modernity. (p. 113)

Taylor, like Connolly, sees the inevitable gaps between our consciousness of the world and that world itself. In addition, he recognizes the structural similarities in apparently contrasting responses to those gaps and the insecurities produced by such gaps. Unlike Connolly, however, Taylor draws on both human anxiety and similarities in cultural responses to that anxiety to argue that unitary ontologies of one sort or another are necessary to human life and thought.

Taylor (1985a) seeks to move beyond such traditional oppositions as reason-nature and community-individual. He attempts to show how both sides of these antinomies share certain assumptions that we must critique and amend if we are to make progress in certain seemingly intractable debates.

Nonetheless, despite Taylor's (1985a) creative efforts to break some familiar bounds, his thought illustrates just how difficult such a process is. He slips beyond his ontological quests into insinuations of concrete absolutes. Taylor seems locked into a set of assumptions about community and moral values held by advocates of radical ecology, industrial growth, and various forms of social democratic sustainability. Though notions of harmony or control or a combination of the two may be inevitable in some form, may we not also interrogate them to determine what they have in common and inquire into the common anxieties from which they emerge?

Is the only answer, the only response to the anxieties Taylor exemplifies, the claim of a unitary truth grounded in some form of idealized nature— albeit a nature, he believes, we cannot ever fully grasp? Could we not learn to accept the unpredictability of nature as grounds for celebration rather than despair? Might we then not be able to use the mystery of life to inspire others and even ourselves to seek more expansive notions of truth and community?

Beyond Holism and Instrumentalism

Jane Bennett (1987) points out in the course of a perceptive critique of both instrumentalist and holistic conceptions of nature that both schools share the sense that nature is made for us. She argues that each side needs the other in another sense as well. The strongest argument on behalf of either seems to be often-cited problems with its opponent. Any holistic orientation argues at least implicitly that any orientation not willing to attach intrinsic value to nature or to impute some direction to it must end in the continual exploitation of it. Instrumentalists argue that any perspective arguing for limits to our ability to understand and manipulate nature is implicitly theological and thereby suspect.

Are there ways of recognizing the limits to our ability to control and manipulate nature without reading teleology into it? Can one adopt a modern understanding of nature without dominating it? Bennett's (1987) critique suggests a portrait of nature that is not only consonant with the social ontology underlying Honig's (1993) work but also with some current strands within scientific ecology. She advocates a picture of *fractious holism*. This ontology suggests a connection among all elements, human and nonhuman, in our world. Each element is constituted by its relation to others. But these patterns and connections are both complex and less than fully determinate. Humans, like every species, need to fashion some structure through their actions in this world; but the very complexity and porousness of the order they inhabit ensure that every action must have consequences that will exceed calculation.

Such a posture recognizes a need for human-centered economic development, but also one that acknowledges aspects of randomness and unpredictability in the natural and human worlds. It therefore argues for allowing maximum feasible natural diversity and reducing one's dependence on far-flung natural resources. This ethic is not grounded on either a form of Darwinism that postulates an automatic balance of nature or a more explicitly teleological valorization of nature.

The work of Foucault (Rabinow, 1984), though not addressed to environmental politics, has clear implications for those who are interested in how notions of community and nature reinforce each other in contemporary sustainability discourse. The key starting point for Foucault is the breakdown of the classical episteme. With the loss of a self-evident order of being and truth, there is a new orientation to difference. Foucault recognizes that the classical or premodern era is not an ideal to which we can or should return. Its conception of order did, however, foster an orientation that discerned secret affinities in apparent patterns of difference between the strange and criminal on the one hand and the more conventional on the other hand. All of that which existed was seen as a part of a larger totality. Even if its assigned place in the order was subordinate and invariant, it nonetheless had a certain ontological warrant.

With the breakdown of the great chain of being and of like ontological schemes, there was an attendant anxiety about the grounding of the social order and a new orientation to difference. The resulting dilemma is nicely articulated by Connolly (1988). There was and is a demand for

> external guarantees inside a culture that has erased the ontological preconditions for them. Modernity is thus an epoch of secret insistence jeopardized by its own legacy of truthfulness and honesty: its bearers demand that every hidden faith be exposed, but faith is necessary to ground the superiority of modern life. (p. 29)

The consequences of the modern situation are well articulated by Romand Coles (1992). Deprived of any firm external foundation for truths, a person must "ceaselessly show that he is the complete foundation of what can be a stable truth, that the unthought can always be thought, that he can seize his origin. Man must attempt to squeeze shut the gaps where the other might arise" (p. 72).

Part of the process of building such an order in which doubt can be suppressed is articulating one whose foundations do not rest on the discredited teleologies of the past. Yet each new order of meaning and value smuggles in unacknowledged elements from its predecessors (see Connolly, 1987, chap. 10). Thus an orderly hierarchy of being gives way to a mechanical universe in which causal regularity and predictability provide the ultimate meaning and security. Furthermore, the modern order's fundamental notion of freedom fails to acknowledge that contemporary conceptions of responsibility—in which persons took upon themselves all blame for evil in the world—emerged out of an effort to free God from responsibility. Nonetheless, despite their best efforts, such perspectives lack the simple unity and clarity claimed for them.

Identity requires differences with and against which it defines itself. There is nothing in the process of identity formation itself that requires that difference be construed as otherness and therefore deserving of contempt, reform, or punishment. Portraying difference in terms of otherness, as something dangerous to our own identity, helps us claim certitude for it. In addition, seeing difference as otherness, as something completely alien to or introduced from beyond the self—even foreign—helps secure that identity against doubt. For if we admit that the other is in some sense a part of us, in what sense can our identity be true?

Thus much modern thought suggests that otherness comes from beyond the self. Homosexuality is often viewed as the product of a bad will or bad training. This not only has implications for injustice, but utterly obscures the dialectic between modern forms of homosexuality and the norms of the society in which they emerge.

The distance from us and fearfulness of the deviant are used to reinforce the established order and values. The other is portrayed as a source of imminent harm. Death, which is no longer portrayed as part of the natural order, is pictured as evil and to be feared or avoided. Fear of death is clearly articulated and intensified as a bulwark of an all-encompassing order, which can give meaning to that death.

A democratic world that professes equality and the individual while leaving little real entree to its opportunities for personal development exacerbates these anxieties. How does a society justify to itself and to its most disadvantaged the harms it will not or cannot redress? How does it justify the social practices that leave so many in desperate poverty? How does it cope with the anxiety and travail even of middle-class citizens coping with the reality of daily life? What better way than to portray those who have not achieved success as part of a genetically, racially distinct—and inferior—group. This group threatens "us," the hardworking strata of middle America. For those whose hold on the American dream of affluence and responsibility is tenuous, both literally and metaphorically taxing, defining those who appear to be outside the disciplines of the system—the hard-core unemployed and the welfare mothers—as inferior to us and the source of our social problems is a persistent temptation. It helps still inner doubts about our own identities and social values.

Today, conceptions of racial difference are used to naturalize the exclusion of certain groups from a level of well-being and dignity that more could achieve. Portraying a culture of poverty as a source of drugs, murder, and starvation stills doubts about what our patterns of growth have brought to all of us. As we shall elaborate in later chapters, the centrality of these exclusive identities lessens possibilities of cooperation in fights to achieve greater social justice for all.

Honig's (1993) reading of such modern communitarians as Michael Sandel is a powerful illustration of this dynamic. Sandel correctly argues that the self cannot be seen as simply immersed and indistinguishable from its instincts, needs, and purposes, but neither can it be seen as completely distinct from these. Against the imagined specter of the self as awash in a plethora of emotions, Sandel pictures the self coming to understand itself as part of a larger but still determinate subjectivity. Through a process of self-discovery that includes the intersubjective dimension of friendship and broader political participation, the individual comes to understand and articulate his or her true selfhood.

Sandel starts from the relatively uncontentious notion that boundaries must constitute individual and collective identity. He moves to the assumption that such boundaries can be fully attuned to the underlying stuff that articulations purportedly clarify. Honig (1993) points out, however, that the mere need for boundaries does not answer the question of how they are to be policed and maintained. Are these boundaries to be contestable and relaxed or rock solid and natural? The doubts occasioned by the evident process of boundary construction are silenced by claiming solidity and finality for those boundaries. That solidity is in turn grounded in the process of consensus building or intersubjectivity. Sandel ultimately privileges his notion of the subject coming to know its own self only in and through community, despite his recognition of the multiple forms that subjectivity can take.

A perspective critical of such holistic ontologies is elicited by a reading of the past and present, a reading of elements of resentment of finitude and indeterminacy implicit in them, of the ways these anxieties have influenced these ontologies. When one is cognizant of these anxieties and the breakdown of previous ontologies, exclusionary perspectives on truth become more transparent and therefore more problematic. Such a reading is not a proof. It is a kind of interpretive exercise that changes our understanding of ourselves. It seeks to elicit in us more appreciation of that in ourselves and others that does not fit favored individual and collective identities.

In this regard, its truth status does not differ fundamentally from the ways in which a range of other teleological doctrines hope to gain our allegiance. The most thoughtful of these have always acknowledged that no ethics can be proven by reliance on rationality itself. All that claim to do so either end up as vacuous or rely on implicit but unacknowledged foundations, as both Charles Taylor (1985a) and Alasdair MacIntyre (1984) forcefully argue. Both postmodern and contemporary teleological perspectives, despite their obvious differences, share a greater self-consciousness as to their own status than their rationalist opponents.

Charles Taylor (1985a) acknowledges that his ethical perspective, just like those of many so-called postmoderns (Connolly, 1992, 1993) is grounded on a fugitive and undocumented source. Nonetheless, Taylor argues that the late modern perspective is far too foreign to have resonance in this society (see Connolly, 1993). We find this view problematic on several grounds.

This posture is arguably latent in many popular discussions of the breakdown of systems and the inevitable failure of reality to live up to ideals. Just as the ethic being advocated here is pluralistic, so are its sources plural. Even within Christian theology, one can read significant instances of concern about the limits of conventional morality.

We believe that much of the best prophetic Protestant theology, inspired in the United States by Reinhold Niebuhr and developed most fully in *The Nature and Destiny of Man* (1964), employs a reading of original sin, God, and *agape* to arrive at an orientation to law very similar to Honig (1993) and Connolly (1987, 1988, 1992, 1993). Niebuhr explicitly rejects a reading of sin in terms of flesh versus spirit or concupiscence. He talks of the ways in which finite human beings absolutize their perspectives in the anxiety of their finitude. Niebuhr ponders questions of punishment and identity. In addition, Niebuhr's picture of God's love as the complete self-giving love displayed by Jesus on the cross is not that of an insidious and ultimately controlling form of love. Rather, it is an acceptance and openness that cannot ever be fully realized in history but that stands in judgment against every historical order or judgment.

Niebuhr (1964) recognizes the element of tragedy in history that stands in stark contrast to both rationalist and communitarian alternatives. The human capacity for good makes democracy possible. The human capacity for evil makes it necessary. Democracy is integral to and made possible by the capacity of human beings to forge purposes beyond themselves. Yet democracy is also needed to counteract the final and all-embracing claims made on behalf of these inevitably partial claims of finality. Humans did not make the world, and absolute claims on behalf of our actual or even potential ability to grasp all within our ethical or cognitive orders are anthropocentric—sinful.

In the contemporary context, Honig (1993) argues that one cannot in the abstract argue the ultimate superiority of a virtù perspective. She highlights forms of resistance and otherness engendered by a range of communitarian and liberal alternatives, which claim at least implicitly they can eliminate the dissonance from social life. She points to the ways in which the magnanimity governing Rawls's famous difference principle is not extended to those whose constitutions cannot be made to fit the rationalism and legalism of the system. Honig points out that Rawls worries about the distribution of income in society, that the least well-off benefit. But he devotes no attention to the questions of the level of punishment—or justification of the same—for those who run afoul of the moral and legal principles of the society.

Honig (1993) makes an analogous analysis for Sandel. Thus, in the area of gay rights, Sandel tries to be more inclusionary through an argument for allowing gay unions. Nonetheless, he grounds this on an exclusion, through his stress on the legal requirement, administered by the government, that to be a good citizen, these relationships must be for life. Surely, boundaries for the moral and legal regulation of sexuality must always exist. Any answer to such questions raises difficult dilemmas, however. Sandel unfortunately forestalls debate by implying that boundaries do not entail loss and need not be periodically monitored, implications that obscure their possible damage.

Work by Honig (1993), Coles (1992), Connolly (1987, 1988, 1992, 1993), Bennett (1987), and others highlights features shared by contending rationalists and holistic environmental schools of thought. From such a perspective, the modern world, from the religious fiefdoms of the Middle East to the advanced "secular" states of the West, is marked by increasing efforts to overcome existential anxiety and discover final and unitary truths. These quests for unitary truths and exclusive identities are themselves provocative of disorder both nationally and internationally.

Furthermore, they either inadvertently or intentionally buttress professional, communal, or autoregulation of the self. Although a range of rationalists like to argue that any perspective suggesting the limits of truth is incoherent, these rationalist critics have in fact assumed the sufficiency of the knowing enterprise and the complete fit between human truths and the world, the very theme under debate here (see Connolly, 1987, chap. 1). In a world in which both discipline and political breakdown grow together, an approach to ecology that places democracy at its core may be more timely. Such work arguably speaks to a part in us that exceeds even the most officially cherished identities fostered in contemporary polities.

Honig (1993), Bennett (1987), and Connolly (1987, 1988, 1992, 1993) are clearly not engaged in the repudiation of political order. Indeed, Honig tries to unsettle the more sedimented readings of the virtù-virtue binary by suggesting that no political order can survive apart from some points of settlement. To suggest that every form of order is equally bankrupt and equally worthy of resistance is itself a form of absolutist politics. In practice, it is a form of escapism or nihilism that voids all politics. Virtù and virtue are necessary moments of social life; each must be kept alive for the sake of the other.

We would prefer to amend or rework this view by suggesting that one can, perhaps must, affirm a direction in human life, but this direction will not be strong or comprehensive enough to embrace all aspects of ourselves. Foucault would argue, something always escapes from or lies outside our necessary efforts to give clarity to this direction. We agree in that we deny that phenomena beyond a favored direction in life are always evil per se, however much any order may have to contain some of them in some fashion. From our perspective, framing purposes and establishing an order with which we can identify is necessary to create the best conditions in modern life for privacy, and individuality. This conclusion becomes clearer once we understand an important dialectic within social life. Without laws that grow out of principles we can understand and at least partially accept, which draw on and articulate this direction within us, we easily resent and resist law and other social requirements as the external impositions they would then be. Such resistance will usually be followed by more intrusive attempts to restore order, especially in times of social change. By the same token, however, those forms of order that fail to acknowledge the limits to these norms and seek to pull too much of the self into their orbit will also occasion destabilizing resistance in some form.

The fight for a realm of privacy, of space not subject to continual regulation and surveillance, is thus necessary to order. Each is a part of and limit to the other, but each is achieved only through a continual process of political contest and adjustment. A final, stable harmony between virtue politics and virtù politics can never be fully encapsulated or negotiated in one neatly formulated truce or policy program. In a world of flux and excess, each new compromise leaves problems or remainders. The perpetual struggle to frame commonalities and respond to the resistances they create is the ineliminable essence of democratic politics. In this context, we would endorse Coles's (1992, 1993) perspective on the fertility of the space between our identity and the other. The common good becomes a social world where different voices can develop in and through, as well as foster, dialogic relations.

Contemporary Individuality and Discourse

In some European countries, it has been suggested that individuals not properly cooperating with recycling and source separation requests have a special ribbon placed on their homes. These displays would subject recalcitrant citizens to peer pressure to cooperate.

A critic might begin by raising the issue of whether simply fining the deviant individual would be more humane than singling him or her out for a public peer evaluation, which might deeply intrude into the reasons one failed to meet such standards.

The consumption of a multitude of products and their ready disposal are deeply ingrained habits. Problematic as those habits may be, they are likely one expression of a certain vitality and variety. Some of that way of life may have to be changed. Nonetheless, the obvious need for recycling initiatives should not be an occasion to hide from scrutiny the harm that any set of policies and sanctions will entail.

One must ask corporate environmentalists whether recycling is intended to facilitate more expanded and unnecessary patterns of consumption by enlarging the pool of cheap resources. In addition, one needs to ask if the burdens of recycling within the home are being disproportionately borne by women.

The risks involved in politicizing a range of relationships lying within the traditional spheres of civil society and the market have led some liberal theorists to argue against their inclusion within any political agenda. Indeed, these theorists see collective political movements as risks not only in terms of the policies that may emerge from them but also the sacrifices to individuality involved in political participation itself. Following Thoreau (see Bennett, 1987), they argue that politics is a realm of the "they" in which the very process of building alliances leads to submersion of individual difference.

Thus George Kateb (1992) can argue that the individuality that Americans cherish is best preserved through the institutions of representative democracy and the market economy. Kateb's work represents a profound celebration of individuality. He is right in pointing to the elements of "homesickness" implicit in many forms of radical democratic politics. The true self, says Kateb, is the alienated self: the self that knows that it is alone and has no final and fixed identity. A broad participatory politics threatens that kind of alienation and tends to exacerbate forms of homesickness, which must be combated.

Such critiques may, however, underplay the way political participation can itself be an arena of surprises in which the limits of the conventional and limits of one's identity become clearer.

Just as fundamentally, liberals in this tradition may be involved in a kind of homesickness of their own. One might argue that positing markets and representative democracy as the primary guarantors of a world of openness constitutes an unacknowledged quest for stability with normalizing implications of its own. Bennett's (1994) work on Thoreau highlights some of the problems implicit in such a perspective. Kateb's ethic can play down the role that isolation can have within the human psyche in promoting forms of radical self-interest that threaten any social order. Just as basically, it "plays down . . . the presence of intractable conflict in the order of things" (p. 89). The space for such grounded and therefore sustainable individuality actually may lie within the interstices of human communities and emerges through cooperation and conflict within the political process. The space itself is never secure or finally established.

Thus, we respectfully differ from Kateb (1992). Our differences involve both history and contemporary political economy. In the first place, whereas Polanyi's (1957) views on premodern communities may neglect the role of power in community formation, his discussions of the history of market societies is compelling. From the late 18th century to today, markets have never been sustained simply by individual choice. The dispossession of people from communal lands in various enclosure movements has been part of the staking out of private property relations.

In addition, we place a different interpretation on consumerism in modern society than many liberals do. Many citizens are left almost entirely outside of modern consumerism and desire access to those goods and services needed to gain entree to a wide range of economic and cultural opportunities. For some others, however, consumerism is at best a mixed blessing. We believe that many people work at long-hour jobs not simply because they seek more personal affluence as a manifestation of their individuality, but because they fear future unemployment, they are compelled, or the nature of the workplace itself forces them to use affluence and personal display as ways to a more fulfilling or less supervised kind of work. Many increasingly resent, at least on some level, the ways in which this consumption treadmill limits time for other pursuits and other venues for human individuality.

Market individualism is a necessary prerequisite of individuality. Still, markets in which unchecked power congeals become a threat to individuality. In this regard, we agree with political theorist Thomas Dumm (1994):

> In his less reflective moments, it is as though Kateb (1992) assumes that all of us are free to dabble in the enormous energies of popular culture and willingly accept the costs involved because we ourselves do not have to pay in boredom, fear of economic dislocation, and the blackmail of conditions. His admirable faith in the capacity of all of us in our own ways to participate in the liberal democratic culture sometimes operates as a rhetoric for evading a confrontation with the most damaging conditions created and sustained by its corporate underpinnings. (p. 33)

Dumm argues that the very propensity to absolutize both individual and collective identities, which we see in many ecofundamentalist movements, may be at least in part a consequence of the exclusions and impositions of corporate culture. Such a perspective suggests the need to see the political nature of markets and the identities and counteridentities that they sustain or engender.

We do not mean to imply by these remarks that the damage imposed by any authority can be undone solely by politics. Collective and individual identities that strive to succeed by exclusion grow and develop within civil society and personal life as well as within politics. Cultivation of a form of selfhood cognizant of the temptations toward and injustices in such forms of identity is also crucial. Bennett's (1994) interpretation of Thoreau is useful here as well. Bennett's exemplary individual, who is attentive to the many sides of his or her being, is crafted through such techniques as periodic withdrawals from social intercourse, episodes of self-induced aphasia, and forms of "microvisioning," where one pays attention to the minutiae of the world and restrains the urge to contextualize or explain what one sees. Artistic creations, by playing off the human longing for connection to a world beyond our immediate experience, can help foster such a self and alert it to the joys made possible by the excesses within ourselves and our world.

Such fabrication of selfhood is both facilitated and impeded by the politics and political economy of this world. A reconstituted politics and sensitivity to the disciplines we impose on ourselves are necessary for and limits to each other. It is our belief that an adequate ecological politics must strive to open up some political space for the discussion of such topics.

Nonetheless, no matter how problematic various contemporary liberal agendas may be, our reading of various ecocommunitarian ones suggests other dilemmas. A full communitarian perspective argues that if there are problems with a standard, communities can resolve these problems by making the community more fair, more inclusive, more clear to everyone. For these communitarians, we can ultimately achieve a full and fully satisfying fit between the demands of the order and the instincts of the self.

We do not deny the need for standards that citizens collaborate in authoring and can come to some understanding of and support for. We do deny that any set of rigid imperatives can ever avoid damage to some groups. Any politicization of the market or related identities, including those we endorse, is not without its risks. The attempt to achieve all-embracing standards that everyone understands and fully accepts will multiply instances of otherness. These will have to be handled through criminalization, therapy, or other disciplines. Another strategy would be to enhance the quality of and adherence to standards by limiting them to the goal of preserving our lives together rather than establishing the truth of our collective and individual identities. Such an ideal is of course imprecise, but no more so than others that guide moral discourse. Its rationale and its contours can only be established through democratic politics.

When we come to recognize that forms of deviation are produced as much by rigid standards as by anything intrinsic to us, we can take a more ironic stance toward that posture. Perhaps we can find ways to foster better kinds of consumption and disposal, even allowing some that are not so good. We can ask how widespread noncompliance is and whether reductions in sanctions would really lead to severe problems. Surely, we can lessen the modes of humiliation we inflict on violators. We also need standards and the stable social and individual identities they enable. The social order constitutes, as well as limits, us. If the world were all chaos, there would be no point in blaming anyone or anything. The goal here simply is to avoid ontologizing standards and identities and treating them as final words no longer in need of either relief or justification.

We must not let apocalyptic narratives about the greenhouse effect or other environmental horrors, however well documented, become an occasion for shutting down the discussion of the harm to some that even solutions entail. Lee Quinby's (1994) *Anti-Apocalypse,* though not focused primarily on environmental issues, is relevant here. Quinby documents the ways in which discursive narratives in politics move from identification of a problem to discussion of the ways in which the problems may putatively contribute to the loss of all social value to definition of those who opposed preferred solutions as intrinsic sources of evil whose voices are to be silenced.

How individual activity that negatively affects the environment must be regulated, with what punishments, with preservation of what opportunities for alternatives, are questions that should always be encouraged within political space rather than excluded by a rhetoric of harmonization, real selves, and the end of civilization. Those who think such examples are fanciful have not lived or worked in some alternative ecological communities where sometimes the urge to establish more sensible ways of life is equaled only by a willingness to humiliate those who cannot fully meet the new norms.

The Body Political

Health requires a new orientation to greater self-reliance that also has ideological implications for the well-being of the body politic. However much the community is a kind of family and the family is a kind of community, to conceive any social structure as an organic unity may be problematic. The move from body to community to family can obscure the metaphorical game going on here. For example, a new health care politics of greater self-understanding and self-reliance is needed. These can also become occasions to aggravate a fear of random or untimely death, however, and with it instantiate greater self-surveillance and a quest for more inclusive orders that give meaning to such lives and deaths.

It is instructive in this regard how a range of ecological movements concerned with slowing the growth imperative instills deeper anxieties and installs pressures for normalization in unintended ways. The move to replace modern high-technology health care with more preventive and "organic" models may be seen in that light. Many of the same groups that endorse a range of community-centered "reduce, reuse, and recycle" strategies also endorse organic modes of health care, the implications of which are worthy of scrutiny. It may well be that their effects on our views of self are more significant than their direct effect on health costs.

As Arney and Bergen (1984) point out, some clinicians today are concerned not simply with organs as such but with their interaction with the individual and social setting. The focus on the patient as a person, an autonomous being able to participate in his or her care, is welcome.

But such attention to the individual in a social setting moves in the direction of fostering norms as to what one does over the whole of one's life. Practitioners of such a perspective seek to implicate the individual, both through education and support groups, in monitoring all aspects of life so as better to fulfill a range of social and economic commitments. Arney and Bergen (1984) eloquently summarize this perspective:

> Put simply, medicine aims for an optimal order. The life span perspective forces medicine to focus on all disruptive and dislocative aspects of life. Disturbances within the relation of the holon hierarchy of systems are problematic, and medicine's task is to restore order. Birth is disruptive. It disrupts a woman's internal organs, the family, the community, and so forth up and down the holon. Death is disruptive. So are problems of adolescence, early adult life, midlife and so on. The new medical logic proposes to meet disruption and dislocation with a policy of "preventive optimization and not only alleviation" which extends over the entire life course. . . . It does not spring into action only as the sick person enters the clinic seeking cure, but it reaches out, locating the person in the community, anticipating problems before they occur, making judgments about the optimal use of limited resources to meet a multiplicity of problems. This policy leaves the physician in a privileged position, but subordinates him to a higher vision than simply health. The physician as well as the patient become subordinate to a vision of order, a generally healthy order, but not an order necessarily based on health. (p. 113)

If one is to watch one's food, one's exercise habits, one's moods, one's friends, and the place in which one lives—with how much room for deviation or error in judgment?—then what sort of a life is it anyway?

"Health," as conventionally defined in some preventive regimes, can too easily become obsessive and consuming routines and an occasion for denying the individual an opportunity to have a range of new experiences and encounters with new environments. As proactive as it seems, it can be a posture of eternal defense.

But as Canguilhem (1991) suggests, humans, both individually and in a collective evolutionary sense, may be capable of developing new parameters of functioning, such as heartbeat and metabolic rates, in response to different cultural and physical challenges. He argues that the concern to avoid all unpredictable situations that might challenge the organism is not

> the general law of life but the law of a withdrawn life. . . . The healthy man does not flee before the problems posed by sometimes hidden disruptions of his habits; even physiologically speaking; he measures his health in terms of his capacity to overcome organic crises in order to establish a new order. (pp. 199-200)

In some of the popular treatises on preventive health, one is told to keep an upbeat attitude in the face of illness and that such an approach is the most important key to wellness. Although there is quite a controversy in the medical literature as to the status of such a claim, we are interested in the social and personal assumptions inside such regimes. One implication is that we are capable of managing our own moods without loss or remainder. Perhaps the person advised to be chipper can act so, but maybe not without hidden resentments about both his or her condition and the advice. The person may be subject to a whole new set of anxieties: Am I really being upbeat enough? Am I believing hard enough that I am going to get better? For those who don't or aren't going to get better, especially those who are relatively young, the obverse of this position is that something is or was wrong with their mind-set, thus authorizing a renewed set of interior mental probings. Surely people seeking hope, or to make peace with their maker, do not need such additional burdens.

Our knowledge of our own bodies and medical science have yielded ways of relieving pain and continuing valued activities longer in our lives. The fact that earlier generations might regard pain or inflexibility in old age as natural conditions is no reason that an era that has found some control and redirection of the human body possible should do so.

Nonetheless, human beings might well question the notion that premature death will ever be a fully preventable condition. Acceptance of this fact may make possible a life of greater freedom and more confident initiatives. We also must question the notion that human beings were designed to achieve a complete fit between mind and body, or the individual and the body politic, or that the mind could be indefinitely reshaped to harmonize with or restore the body.

That rejecting certain preventive techniques or lifestyle changes may drive up health costs for others or that premature death robs one's family and friends are surely preeminent values. Nevertheless, we should be concerned about the continued medicalization of life and the way this not only continually reminds one of his or her mortality but also implicitly treats this mortality as punishment for one's improprieties.

We can see, therefore, that the implications of health care go beyond questions of the amount of money we spend on the ill—important as that is. These relate to the conception of self and of the relation of the self to the community that various metaphors of the body instantiate into our discourse. Fears of premature death may exaggerate anxieties and foster certain modes of normalization that extend beyond our own personal well-being but that harm the well-being of others. In Chapter 7, we come back to a discussion of the ways in which a modern ecology program can become an occasion for imperialistic forays into the self.

Metaphors of the healthy body from the world of various medical texts surely play a subtle role in influencing these discourses. The irony is palpable. As some holistic practitioners seek to free us from the autocracy of medical science, they run the risk of interiorizing an alternative autocracy within our very selves. Health care is emblematic of larger trends within the body politic.

The problem is that new modes of travel, energy production and use, health care, consumption, and waste disposal cannot be successfully handed down from on high. Such policies require some change of mind-set on the part of a substantial sector of the population, but the very need for and success in achieving such changes tends to naturalize them, to lead us to see these as basic to the way things really are.

In the context of such scientifically and socially perplexing questions, a politics along the lines we are commending will never end; we would be the better for its continuation. As workers and citizens change their outlooks and actions in response to new standards, the polity must make periodic adjustments both to meet widely perceived needs and to keep the pain adjustments bring to some to a minimum.

Political settlements often leave some hurts and disappointments, and problems and discontents congeal over time. Nonetheless, though there are no guarantees in political life, political orders that seek to limit the damage of regulation and implicitly accept the right and need to politicize even good regulations are more likely to engender more decency. As Honig (1993) would argue, advocates of such a perspective on law and policy are engaged in a wager that a set of arrangements and orientations that chasten aspirations to final closure will produce less resistance and more political legitimacy. If such a wager fails, it has the advantage of producing more politics than one might want, rather than more punishment that one should fear.

An ecofundamentalist stance within the polity not only risks damaging individuals but also severely limits the possibilities of broad coalitions and long-term political legitimacy. This is not to suggest that ecofundamentalist ideas are unimportant or simply wrong. Their views are an essential screen against which we project our own.

One suspects that the invocation of local communities in these ecofundamentalist texts is intended to give environmental law the imprimatur of the long-established, harmonious community from which we all presumably sprang. In the process, however, it paradoxically downplays the permanent need for politics if reasonable spaces for community autonomy are to be fashioned. Just as problematically, such a strategy makes it more difficult to mitigate the elements of exclusion that inevitably go into community formation. What we must resist is their conception of all-embracing absolutes and the accompanying, if unintended, denigration of politics.

The attempt to build community consensus around regulations, necessary to modern life, is important if such regulations are to be followed widely. Nonetheless, every consensus represents in part an accidental and temporary construction rather than expression and clarification of totally unifying essences. Foucault (Rabinow, 1984) summarizes this orientation nicely, and his view provides an interesting comparison and contrast with Bookchin (1985). In a discussion of consensuality and the modern world, Foucault remarked, "The farthest I would go is to say that perhaps one must not be for consensuality, but that one must be against nonconsensuality" (cited in Bennett, 1987, p. 217; Dumm, 1988, discusses this famous remark). Foucault is suggesting that in our necessary quest for better and more acceptable moral schemes, for solutions to our practical social problems, we may blind ourselves to the limits of all solutions, limits that spring not merely from the partial and incomplete information with which we must always work but also from the lack of fit between the world and the human subject.

We must have some order to our world. Far better that this order come from our common participation and free acquiescence. Nonetheless, as Dumm (1988) so cogently puts it,

Foucault refused to place consensuality, whether actual or ideal, beyond criticism because it contains artifice, blurs the contingency of its own truth, and participates in the defeat of otherness. If one refuses the blackmail of being compelled to choose between the two, one can then ironize consensus by pointing to its dependence on a larger coercion, even as one opposes nonconsensus based on a more explicit use of force.

The invocation of community allows ecopopulists to avoid the charge of big government. Nonetheless, the coercions of political life stalk even their narratives. Perhaps the best intervention into the discourse of environmental politics is to admit these dangers and constitute democratic politics to address them. We might then reconstitute government as a better medium to extend opportunities for participation and self-development. In the process, we must also strive to open up cultural and political space for criticism and limitation of the burdens that even a constructive agenda must entail.

5 Principles of Sustainability

Equality, Growth, and Political Crisis

Economic growth creates environmental problems. But must this be so? Must conventional economic growth remain an imperative we can neither live with nor without? Is there a way to have an equitable, robust economy without harming the ecology on which it depends?

The U.S. economy seems at an impasse today. Increasingly, it competes in an international free trade environment that forces firms to lower per unit costs even while it propels many large ones to disperse their activities internationally. Many thrive in this international economy. The Dow Jones Industrial Average continually sets "new highs."[1] Yet economic growth along current lines seems only to have exacerbated the social inequities that have characterized so much of our history. Many companies prosper and "downsize." Others merge (still others split) and downsize. Competition often is fierce.

A large underclass of racial minorities, single mothers, and poor whites needs higher incomes to provide for their children or to achieve access to the most minimal requisites of effective citizenship. A larger middle and working class finds itself increasingly squeezed in its efforts to achieve security and self-respect. There seem to be two alternatives: Expand the pie so that all can prosper, a prospect that seems to recede as postindustrialization and globalization create wider inequities, or demand sacrifices of other embattled constituencies and resist their calls for government help.

An ironic political impasse is created. Popular attitudes are far more supportive of environmental protection than they have been in the past.

Nonetheless, competitive pressures on firms and individuals temper support for an environmentally sustainable agenda. Debate instead remains focused on how to "grow" the economy in unsustainable ways or on how to protect one's income from the demands of "unproductive" others. This derivative of contemporary political economy is a formula for continued environmental decay and social injustice.

Yet as the quality of life erodes and real income stagnates, each strategy solidifies. Consider some of the effects of stagnating real wages and the failure of previous reforms during the last 25 years. They hurt the poor most while stiffening the resistance of the working and middle classes to redistributive programs. They have reinforced an underclass and have made the underclass and the government, which seems to some to create it, targets of discontent—thereby reconstructing racial, ethnic, and antigovernment stereotypes. They have fostered *unreflective* support for progrowth economic policies such as repeal of the Endangered Species Act, which may destroy economically significant biodiversity and thus harm both economy and environment. Meanwhile, jobs and income have been lost to cheap labor and environmentally destructive foreign producers.

As income stagnates and jobs become less secure, some seek private solutions, such as working longer hours. These "solutions" yield a deteriorating quality of life because people have less time to spend with their families or in leisure pursuits. They devalue the civic commitments required to address environmental and other problems.

Environmental politics thus plays itself out in a context of slow growth, deepening socioeconomic inequality, and increased racial, ethnic, and gender tensions. This context slows the development of an economically productive—and just—response to ecological decline. An adequate analysis must consider carefully these related phenomena and a plausible agenda must respond to the dilemmas they spawn. Agenda and analysis alike need to pay special attention to the role of government, including theoretical analysis of the role of the modern liberal welfare state. Government is the screen against which many people still project both their aspirations and their resentments. In addition, government in a democracy is one place where the average person can have some say in the direction that large impersonal forces take, whether of politics, economics, quality of life, or environmental crisis. Moreover, the modern welfare state, as conceived by Franklin Roosevelt and his associates, is the locus of the ideological formula that the tensions formed around class (as well as racial, ethnic, and gender) divisions can be adequately salved with the remedy of economic growth. Understanding the government's deficiencies, therefore, is environmentally, politically, and economically necessary.

What direction should political reforms take? The essence of reform is to change business as usual, but to change it in a way that is based on the culture of the society. Not to do so is to fail politically or to call for real (or imagined) revolution, which then requires a moral defense of the scope of the changes entailed—and the price that must be paid for them. We do not believe such a defense can be given.

The question of direction is an appropriate one, but it requires consideration of another question. How can we conceive of political reform so as to avoid some of the traps in which previous movements have found themselves? We can begin by considering the reality that movements for reform, like all movements, do not grow in a vacuum. Proper understanding of them, their strengths and their weaknesses, requires situating them in time, place, and thought.

The most salient reform movements in the United States have been shaped within the contractarian philosophy and practice of liberal capitalism. That tradition pictured a political state as a creature fashioned to protect and legitimate what was viewed as a "natural" private order composed of civil society (the realm of private property relations, religion, culture) and the family (the heterosexual unit for reproduction and nurturing of future citizens and workers). In the original form, men entered into a social contract to get out of the state of nature; this contract entailed submitting to the rules of both civil society and the state. But equality of rights for all men was guaranteed in the state, and natural rights, such as the rights of life, liberty, and property, were protected from the state.

In reality, this social contract has always been stained with inegalitarian relations of gender, class, and race. Indeed, present relations of power are both a product of and remain sustained by such inequalities. Nevertheless, pushed hard by political dissidents to fulfill the logic of its credo (or a logic that could plausibly be derived from it), this tradition was transformed. In its modern version, the Lockean tradition guarantees all citizens equality before the law regardless of ascriptive characteristics.

Similarly, the Lockean tradition (discussed in Kuehls, 1996) has been extended with regard to the natural roles of government, civil society, and families. Here the results are ideologically more ambiguous. Power over others derived from private property has for some time been at a scale hardly imagined by Locke. The government has taken over many more responsibilities for social welfare, for shaping the political culture, and for financially supporting the private economy than Locke considered. The modern expanded government may have been brought more in line with the inherent tendencies of Locke's overall view if not with his own 17th-century predilections. In addition, the family spends less time in direct economic activities and more time and effort preparing its members for economic activity. Within these changing parameters, however, the roles assigned to family members, business, and government still are seen as natural and they continue to be naturalized in contemporary political discourse.

Thus the natural roles assigned to various societal institutional practices and the focus on the contractarian ideology of equality before the law continue to dominate contemporary politics, including the kinds of proposals reformers make. Unfortunately, they may often militate against our ability to solve some of the problems we have identified.

Rights, Principles, and Objectives

A number of contemporary theorists and activists would correct many of the wrongs in American society by turning to government to protect and extend rights now imperfectly supported.[2] For example, they believe affirmative action effectively asserts a real right to equal opportunity in professional jobs for all women and minorities. In a racist and sexist society, they argue, rights so conceived are a necessary, concrete form of protection.

Talk of this sort has a strong moral basis and is indissolubly linked to American political culture. As with the civil rights movement, it is a plausible strategy because it represents an effort to extend important American principles to certain classes of citizens who do not fully share in what these principles claim all citizens should enjoy. The principle of equal opportunity implies that all have a right to it. Affirmative action is a medium through which to make that right actionable.

Some advocates of this position, however, do not consider fully other social consequences that flow from unqualified acceptance of these principles. Exclusive focus on rights talk reinforces a notion of society as a zero-sum game and helps legitimize some of the very principles that make such talk necessary. Equal opportunity is certainly a fair way to construct a regime of competition for society's scarce rewards. Construed simply as making a race fairer, however, it does little to mitigate the harshness of the competition itself. A society in which winners and losers are determined without any reference to ascriptive characteristics would be a fairer society but it would be no less competitive. In fact, in one way, it would become more competitive. No one would have any excuse for failure and all would interpret low status or reward as personal inadequacy rather than as a consequence of prejudice.

The rights talk that emanates from the principle of competition in the first instance lends legitimacy to it.[3] Rights talk of this sort also naturalizes both a particular notion of government and a particular notion of persons. The government is seen as the guarantor of rights within liberalism, as extended to the idea of the welfare state in the Roosevelt and Johnson administrations. Yet it implies an even more bureaucratic and litigious state than we now have; how could such a state sustain the burden placed on a rights agenda to solve the country's major problems? The competitive, inegalitarian, and zero-sum order is a sure catalyst of disobedience to law, evoking continual monitoring, resistance, and repression.

As Wendy Brown (1995) demonstrates, the politics of rights is also tethered to philosophical liberalism at the level of the individual psyche. It grew up out of a sense of the individual as emancipated from all premodern notions of natural hierarchy or chains of being. But that individual, now alone in a world no longer anchored to a higher purpose, has not shaken off the need to order that world either through mastery or through understanding of its inner purposes and direction. Out of such concerns is born the modern liberal conception of the person as autonomous and rational, a being who sees himself or herself as able to bring all aspects of its psyche under standards that he or she can endorse on reflection. This kind of person and this kind of government, however, are problematic and at the same time give cause for hope. The hope lies in the conviction that society should be made to operate fairly and that autonomous agents are the ones who, through their government, can insist on such fairness.

Problems accrue, however, when we consider that this kind of person, with the decline of traditional society, must structure and discipline himself or herself both physically and psychologically. Furthermore, to the extent that he or she evades such disciplines, guilt may be experienced and relieved by projecting forbidden desires onto others and using the state to discipline them. As a sense of gaps and excesses within ourselves and others deepens, anxiety is also experienced, motivating broader needs for certainty as to who one is—and who the other is not—and greater self-control and control of the other.

If questions within oneself about how hard one works provoke anxiety about what one is doing with one's life, one kind of resolution is to construct a class of others who seem to be evading the disciplines one endures and to discipline them to resolve one's own guilt. As an individual blames some people for not doing their share, he or she may broaden the net too widely: The blue-collar worker may also capture within the net of "welfare cheat" some constituencies that might have become worthwhile allies in an effort to improve his or her own life. He or she then elects governments that discipline potential allies. An unintended consequence of such a political practice is to reinforce views of persons and government that undermine the possibility of coalitions for effective change (DeLuca, 1995).

Contrary to some contemporary liberal theorists, we argue that rights are most politically efficacious not when they are concrete and highly specific but when they grow out of widely shared aspirations and provide a basis for as full individuality as possible for all. The right to vote was won through political struggle, but a struggle that could appeal to aspects within the widely held liberalism of its day. It created emancipation at the time of enactment, extending the core ideas of liberalism into greater conformity with ideals of democracy. In the process, a superior political order was created, that of liberal democracy. The gains implicit in that right allowed all citizens to reshape and limit constraints in their lives.

To illustrate, let us discuss the relationship between markets and families. No social order could endure without the nurturing of the young by those who put children's needs above material accumulation. One important task of the family is to impart such an orientation to moral and social value. Liberalism in the past relegated women to the private realm, that of nurturers, and left this role outside political debate. However, such naturalization of women's roles occurring in a society breaking free of the moorings of more traditional worldviews still opened the possibility that women too might consider themselves capable of citizenship and demand it. As liberal society matured, more and more women questioned this role.

If the contemporary market is construed simply as natural, its propensity to exacerbate patterns of inequality as differentially situated persons and corporations compete is elided from political discourse. Yet, as Milton Friedman (1962) argues, ascriptive inequalities are inconsistent with efficiency and, therefore, with market principles. This is important because, although Friedman errs in believing competition will naturally lead the market to become fairer socially, his analysis implicitly raises the question as to whether present markets are the only kind imaginable within market ideology. We suggest that treating present markets as the only conceivable kind of market "naturalizes" them and blinds us to other possibilities.

Now let us consider an example of the kind of problem naturalizing markets and families in this way creates. On the one hand, we rightly celebrate the moral, social, and educational role of the family, whereas on the other we too easily countenance the forces eroding the family. The quest for economic survival of the family and gender justice today often requires entry into the market by women. Yet because the role of women as nurturers and the power relations exhibited by contemporary markets are often naturalized in political discourse, women's participation in this public arena is not properly compensated nor is the arena made suitable for those who must meet critical nurturing responsibilities—whether women or men. Within liberal society, one finds institutions of family and markets that society values but that seem to undermine one another. Because society has failed properly to scrutinize each, it becomes more obtuse to the way that naturalization is part of the problem. Do conceptions of markets and families exist that can better support one another?

We suggest that it is fruitful to denaturalize concepts such as autonomous individuals, families, and markets to see how they can be thought about in ways that preserve the more generous reasons we are so strongly committed to them in the first place. Discussion of rights is a good place to begin. Rights must grow out of broadly based commitments if they are to be acceptable and effective. We believe there are at least five such rights consistent with sustainability principles and objectives and American political culture.

First, we think all Americans should have a right to a real opportunity to work of the kind only a full employment economy can provide and the right to organize within the workplace for greater responsibilities and powers there.[4] Second, all Americans should have the right to family integrity and leisure time, including the right to decide autonomously how much and when to work and the right to basic security in childhood and old age. Third, to control government policy, citizens need a right to *real* political equality, political equality in fact as well as theory (DeLuca, 1995). Fourth, to control the market, consumers require a right to information, education, and protection regarding product, production process, and technology development. Fifth, to control international trade, workers and citizens need the right to open negotiation of trade treaties that extend these rights into the international economy.

However, rights talk alone elides questions of the good of the larger community. To assure the broadest notion of rights that will really help free us, we need to develop sustainable principles and objectives of development that can create the kind of ecologically sensitive and socially just society we aspire to. Wishing society to behave better does not suffice if we do not have motivational and organizational practices that can make society work. We can claim all the rights we want. If our claims contradict existing modes of economics and politics, however, we run the risk of having them discredited by a popular opposition more in tune with the way piecemeal changes countervene structural constraints. By deriving such rights, principles, and objectives from the reexamination of existing ones, we imply that change can be made in the foreseeable future, democratically by ourselves and our children.

We believe these rights and the principles and objectives we now discuss, would constitute a positive intervention in political life, but part of their efficacy lies in the means they afford us both to revise the principles themselves and to combat their excesses. No one set of principles, rights, or policies automatically secures the reconstruction of key institutions in ways that ensure the widest possible scope for human individuality. The idea that our suggestions should become a new orthodoxy is inconsistent with our earlier claims about the intrinsic need for democratic deliberation and consideration to avoid the dangers all forms of naturalization create. To make grand claims for our views not only casts a veil over the flux of life and is unavailing, it feeds and grows on the very process of guilt creation and self- and social regimentation that creates a psychological barrier against fuller democracy. Nonetheless, a different orientation to politics and policy can emerge from consideration of the possibilities and limits of these suggestions.

Five principles are important in creating sustainable democracy in today's world. They could become building blocks for greater individuality as they provide the basis for more democracy, more consensus around solutions achieved democratically, and the self-confidence that effective, fair solutions bring.

First, an efficient, productive, equitable economy and a national commitment to corporations that seriously engage in sustainable development is necessary. Second, a political system that encourages all citizens to participate in the public sphere and that allows them real input into deliberations such as these, is needed. Third, a culture committed to enhancing quality of life is vital. Fourth, an economic and political system, and culture, committed to making ecological sustainability an item within the range of choices available to all persons, must exist. Fifth, all nations that make serious efforts to subscribe to the above four principles should be our primary partners in free-trade agreements.

These principles are in the best traditions of American society and reform movements. They are not, however, as self-evident as they seem. Our present market is not as equitable, efficient, or productive as it might be, nor does it make the best use of its workers. The planning and development that sustainability requires can be very profitable in the long run, but short-term profit taking, especially given the speed of contemporary financial markets, can undermine such planning. Political equality formally exists, but in practice the potential influence of citizens—even of equally talented citizens—is widely disparate. We talk about declining quality of life, but we measure progress by indicators of gross material growth, which only measure gross economic productivity. As workers, consumers, family members, or community residents, we need to be making more choices about—and be in a position to take more responsibility for— the environment we are part of. Lastly, the concerns expressed above become economically and politically difficult to achieve—even if we desire them—if other nations violate their canons, thereby exploiting people and resources in ways that put our economic actors at a competitive disadvantage.

These principles do suggest objectives toward which policymakers should strive. First, we need to readjust the kinds of subsidies we grant through tax dollars to major corporations to facilitate a transition to sustainable technologies. Conservatives today like to talk about eliminating the government role in economic development. Yet the tax code is rife with subsidies to the petrochemical industries in their many manifestations. Oil depletion allowances have long aided the oil industry. Much agricultural policy has long been an enormous subsidy to large, high-tech, petrochemical-intensive farms. Eliminating these subsidies would not, by itself, adequately address these problems. The long period of federal subsidy has made talk of a level playing field a joke. We must give ecological technologies at least as much support as conventional technologies have received. In this way, we can prevent the use of environmentally destructive production processes and products without undermining the profitability and competitive position of firms. We also concomitantly need to limit the need for a large federal bureaucracy engaged in microregulation. Here the work of Barry Commoner (1990) is very important.

Second, we need to develop policies to encourage corporations to engage in long-term planning and to develop tools to limit quick profit taking through financial transactions that discourage corporate planning and sometimes undermine productive companies. Important gains in sustainability can be achieved in the relative short run, but a substantial sustainability orientation will require planning for the long term and national commitments to businesses that engage in such planning.

Third, productivity gains can be encouraged in humane ways by improving the quality of work life, thereby enhancing employee commitment to work. Work life quality improvements, in turn, entail greater employee participation in product choice, design, and production; greater say over the conditions of work; and more responsibility for monitoring work life and product safety and the sustainability of the overall production process. Increased worker participation can protect sustainability by allowing people closest to the work process, and often the first victims of health, safety, and environmental problems caused by it, to become partners in environmental protection.

Fourth, greater equity is also required both for sustainability and for justice. The United States today has greater income and wealth inequality than any other advanced industrial nation (Wolff, 1995). The best single thing we can do to combat these inequities is to create a full employment economy. One step we can take in that direction is to reward workers for productivity gains through higher wages, while allowing them to reward themselves by choosing reduced hours. Although this step allows some workers to get off the treadmill of work and spend, reducing demand, it allows others to achieve incomes that enable them to purchase products necessary for a reasonably high quality of life.

Great inequality also exists due to racial, ethnic, and gender injustices, which also would be mitigated by full employment. Affirmative action and strong civil rights enforcement are important because full employment by itself will not produce equitable employment or pay equity. For reasons of fairness as well as politics, affirmative action should be designed carefully to focus on helping those from families with persistent historic disadvantages, perhaps even those that do not stem from race and gender injustice. In this way, we can begin to blunt affirmative action's use as a wedge issue to divide constituencies most likely to support this agenda.

In addition, postindustrialism and the importance placed on education suggest that much greater equity is required across the board in educational opportunity and higher standards must be set for achievement. With greater participation at work, education will more effectively enhance productivity. Along with full employment, it will ease the pressures for education to be regarded as a vehicle of competition rather than one of individual development.

Greater equity has direct environmental benefits. A more educated public with a higher median income puts consumer, employee, community, and political pressure on business and government to produce a more habitable environment. For example, to the degree programs for equity lessen the feminization of poverty, women from such homes become more effective political and economic actors. Their children begin life with less educational, health, and economic disadvantages, positioning them better to protect their own environments. By developing political processes to eliminate environmental racism, for example, we make cost displacement of hazards far more difficult. This increases the cost of unsustainable technologies and creates an incentive to displace them.

Fifth, more effective political participation requires recognition of the gap that exists between formal or legal equality in the voting booth, and real political equality. Political equality is necessary to ensure that the role government will have to play in creating an environmental future is as even-handed and as little onerous as possible. Equality here is in the tradition of the best impulses of American political development and consistent with the logic of our cultural heritage. Although real political equality is an ideal that surely never will be attained fully, we can achieve greater equity in political resources and decision making.

Many proposals have been made to achieve this end. The correlation between our extraordinarily low rates of electoral participation and socioeconomic status and education indicate a profound bias in the present system. Higher participation would indicate a mitigating of political inequality. This result could be accomplished by making voting easier and by expanding the political agenda to encompass the needs of those to whom Walter Dean Burnham refers as the "party of nonvoters" (see DeLuca, 1995). Political alienation even among voters indicates that many feel the system does not fairly respond to their needs and must be reformed. These objectives could be facilitated by adopting a system of automatic universal registration of voters. We should also simplify our complex array of election schedules and political offices. Improving the quality and equity of our educational systems and the media dispensing information to us would spark voter interest. Implementing a system of proportional representation, eliminating the role of money in politics through public financing of elections, and placing tighter controls on the corrupting influences of lobbyists would also dramatically improve access for the average voter (DeLuca, 1995).

Sixth, we need to develop qualitative economic measures and use them as indicators of present performance and guides for future planning. It is absurd, for example, that our key guide to economic performance, gross national product (GNP), goes up when companies are taken over by corporate raiders who then dismantle them, costing us jobs and products while disrupting communities. Even more scandalous, when corporations produce cleanup techniques whose sole purpose is to remove the pollutants of other production processes, GNP goes up. Herman Daly and John Cobb (1989) develop an innovative index of sustainable economic welfare that is far superior to conventional GNP accounting. Daly and Cobb consider depletion of scarce resources, environmental pollution, and the degree of social inequality factors that add to the cast of human needs. The Commerce Department would do well to take account of these in devising a more sensitive measure of total national product.

Seventh, as a society, we need to ask a very important question that we seem to have forgotten. For years, business and professional leaders have told us that automation will lift us out of a life of drudgery. Many innovations have eased physical burdens. Nevertheless we find ourselves working harder today than at any time in the last quarter century (Schor, 1991). Why is automation not meeting the claims of its advance billing? The reasons are complex, including the treadmill of spend and work, harder work driven by international competition among firms, short-term profit taking, increasing gaps in incomes and wealth, and limited rights of workers to choose leisure rather than overtime pay. We need substantial discussions of how to derive maximum qualitative benefits from automation while minimizing economic problems generated.

Qualitative measures of performance also imply a need for qualitatively superior and sustainable technologies and products. Much of our work here is designed to bring about just this result. Decisions about quality are always controversial; we think they should be made democratically in two ways: through the market by informed consumers and through the political process by politically equal citizens.

Eighth, we need to give greater consideration to ways we can augment sustainable consumption. To do so effectively, it may be necessary to think about organizing at the point of consumption. Consumers who demand things that really improve the quality of their lives and reject things that detract from them could revolutionize the production system. This would require a level of consumer information and organization nowhere yet achieved, however. Political organizing to control negative consequences of business practices has often occurred at the point of production through unions. As business becomes more mobile and as many businesses downsize, however, worker security becomes more tenuous. In addition, people today identify themselves as much as consumers as employees. Consumer unions of various sorts have existed for some time, as have organizations that inform the public about the need to buy green products. These just scratch the surface of what a concentrated program of sustainable consumption could achieve, however.

Ninth, all this becomes more practical if we adjust our trade policies. Expanded trade can have wonderful economic benefits; by increasing interdependence, it can limit xenophobia and lessen the possibility of war. However, when trade only benefits certain segments of society it can be one catalyst for reactions that have exactly the opposite effect. A race with firms relocating in quest of cheap labor drives wages down everywhere and undermines the purchasing power that sustains employment. Moreover, when we trade with nations that do not follow sustainability principles, we expand their pool of capital through which to exploit further the environment and often their own people. We also put economic pressure on our own businesses and political actors to join in rejecting sustainability principles. Trading with nations that violate workers' rights abroad creates economic opportunities for our own firms to leave and undermines employee power in the work process. Free trade does not have to exist only between nations at equal levels of political and economic development. Nonetheless, for it to be really free, it must exist primarily with nations that fairly treat their citizens and regard their environment smartly.

Tenth, we need to consider how we view our ideas about national citizenship and patriotism. American constitutional design, and supportive landmark Supreme Court decisions (e.g., *Gibbons v. Ogden*) have established the union of states as a free trade zone and a national political economy (DeLuca, 1995 chaps. 1 and 3). Although this has produced many positive benefits, it creates a recurring issue that is not often considered systematically. Any state or local government that adopts policies unpopular with or unresponsive to important segments of the business community puts itself at a competitive disadvantage with states that do not do so. Democratically elected local and state governments are continually under pressure to adjust these to the needs of private economic actors (Kantor, 1995), although state governments operate from a stronger position than local ones.

Moreover, environmental problems are no respecters of state, city, or county borders. For these reasons the most essential (although not the only) aspects of sustainability programs must be enacted, after extensive local and state consultation, by democratically elected representatives at the national level. Administration could be devolved to the state and local levels, although the state level is preferable because it can more easily protect the integrity of the program. Clear procedures must be in place to mitigate implementation that, in practice, would be biased or in other ways compromise the standards set. When America's real national security is threatened, we respond as a nation and ask all to shoulder equal burdens. Morally and practically, a similar idea of national citizenship is necessary to improve the quality of life of Americans, to preserve our resources, and to enhance our system's sustainability.

In arguing for an essential role for government, we do not suggest that government is not in need of extensive reforms. In the next chapter, we suggest reasons why government's role is essential and why and how government needs to be reformed. Flexible but firm government action will remain necessary in the areas of subsidies, tax incentives, regulation, prevention, and monitoring. But government must do its job better, partly by becoming more innovative and more accountable democratically and partly by being freed from the illicit ways its work is undermined.

The objectives and proposals we suggest throughout this book do not depend only on governmental reform, however. There is no faith here in government as the solver of all our problems. We need a panoply of enlightened business practices, empowered and informed consumers, communities more able to defend themselves, employees held in higher regard, and more effective democracy to discipline government itself. Business will have to look less at the quarterly bottom line and more at long-run, responsible profitability. Employees, consumers, and community residents need to be in a position to take more responsibility for what they do or what they countenance. More effective political equality can help us pursue these requirements with legitimacy and commitment as a national community. Each of these objectives makes the others more likely to succeed and to be embraced. Conceived in this way, sustainability both builds political support for itself and ensures that the program limits, to the greatest degree possible, the impositions institutions put on us in its implementation.

The above list of rights, principles, and objectives is not meant to be exhaustive but it does highlight the main features of an environmentally sound agenda that is both fair and democratically sustainable. Such an agenda is dependent on Americans as a people being in a position to decide for themselves what they consider to be an optimum quality of life and to choose what they decide.

Markets and Sustainability

These rights, principles, and objectives are essential components of a just, sustainable ecological agenda. They help secure that agenda from political and economic intimidation while building a broad constituency for it. Furthermore, gains in these areas would give citizens the means to contest impositions on their individuality—even those undertaken in the name of the agenda itself. In this sense, it is first and foremost a statement of democratic rights.

This reform agenda not only would foster ecological sustainability, it would also make the market economy and therefore its society more stable. An agenda that gives workers the right to move toward a greater share of ownership and workplace input and places a floor under worker wages through regulation of their hours will provide more insurance that demand keep up with rising productivity. It will also foster a broader and more democratic form of entrepreneurialism. Demand will tend to remain high relative to production because workers can keep wages high and hours shrinking. In addition, a market economy in which workers have an ownership stake will foster the ability and willingness—as well as the need—to take some of the proceeds from strong sales and invest in new technologies essential for their own place of work. Firms that choose to rest on their laurels will face substantial competitive pressure.

Such an economy will be more able to avoid the two most common paths to economic downturn faced by contemporary market economies (Bowles & Edwards, 1993). Recessions are always the result of long-term profit squeezes. Profits may be squeezed by sluggish worker incomes that fail to keep pace with increases in productive capacity. They may also be squeezed in high-employment economies when workers who have no stake or interest in their jobs take advantage of their bargaining position to demand such high wages that nothing is left over for long-term productive investment. In such a context, employers stop investing in new technologies and productivity slows even if government can sustain full employment policies.

The full agenda we propose will foster a society more innovative and stable than most existing market economies. Firms in such an economy will be competing to supply whatever level of products—and level of overall safety—society has settled on in as productive a fashion as possible. Large firms will continue to emerge, but where their market strengths do not yield enhanced productivity and innovation, the public will now have the power to press for investment in new technology.[5] Cyclical ups and downs can be limited without having to resort to stimulation of consumption through government pump-priming programs. Government will still have a role to play in enforcement and social investment, but spending simply for the sake of stimulating consumption by others will be greatly reduced.

The cyclical nature of most unregulated market economies drives unnecessary and unfulfilling forms of consumption. The need and desire for endless growth in material goods will be less driven by status needs in the workplace, extreme inequalities, the lack of social goods, or the extreme insecurities of the order. Supply will be limited through social and personal choice of hours, and demand and productivity will be maintained by worker power in the workplace and the polity. This is one route to the kind of steady state capitalism John Stuart Mill (1965) envisioned more than a century ago.

Notes

1. During part of the time in which we wrote this book, February 1995 through June 1996, the Dow Jones Industrial Average went from under 4,000 to 5,700, an increase in net worth for capital of 42%.

2. Political magazines on the Left are full of defenses of affirmative action. This is not surprising nor is it inappropriate. What is more surprising is how little attention these magazines devote to the ways the U.S. political economy squeezes working-class citizens and sets up this zero-sum conflict. Many on the Left seem to have given up hope of substantial reform of the political economy and are striving only to gain a better piece of the action for those they regard as most disadvantaged. We doubt that such a strategy can prevail. A typical example of celebration of affirmative action amid a decreased attention to socioeconomic class and the larger political economy is Wilkins (1995).

3. We say here in the first instance because once ascriptive issues are eliminated, it may become easier to focus on the question of "opportunity for what?" Thus equal opportunity can become more than a competition for resources or status. It can become a striving for fair distribution of the requirements for a good *quality* of life.

4. This right does not extend to those who show by their behavior that they refuse to take advantage of the opportunity. Although society may eventually move toward more universal forms of income protection, ensuring job opportunities for all is a good place to start within the current modes of work life and culture.

5. The whole subject of bigness and industrial policy is complicated. Suffice it to say, we believe that large corporations can serve the public good through long-term planning, innovation, and economies of scale. They can also use their power to blunt competition and receive monopoly profits. In an economy with more information about corporate behavior, the public can take appropriate action, such as by encouraging competition or new product development. The notion of subsidies and a research consortium to develop alternatives to a gasoline powered vehicle is an important instance of an ecological industrial policy. Industrial policy is more fully elaborated in Buell (1995) and Best (1990).

6 Directions for Future Policy

Ecology and Social Policy

The rights, principles, and objectives discussed in the previous chapter are also consonant with widely held views within American reform traditions and political culture. The United States is portrayed by many—across the political spectrum—as the preeminent liberal society in which the market is king. Nonetheless, as Theda Skocpol (1995) demonstrates, interventions in the market have gained long-term support when they were broad-based and accorded with widely held moral notions. The Civil War pension plan was an innovation adopted to reward military service, just as social security was designed to protect the end of a life of work in the 20th century.

Today, for example, some form of child allowance coupled with automatic attachment of income of the noncustodial parent in the case of divorce could gain a real political presence. These policies could both ease economic insecurities and temper the divisiveness surrounding the politics of welfare.[1]

To finance some of the programs required by a sustainability agenda and to promote even more independence and personal development, the United States would require the stability and tax base provided by universally available decent jobs at a living wage. Skocpol (1995) points out, however, that politics organized around the concept of class has usually been a nonstarter in our society. Our polity is decentralized; citizens think of themselves in regional terms. Despite the lack of a clearly articulated class politics, Americans have often been receptive to the notion that government has a responsibility to give citizens an opportunity for self-development and economic advancement. A program of opportunity for full employment would be one such program.

Within the context of our decentralized polity, we could meet such a commitment through community prioritizing of local needs and federal grants to localities to meet those needs. Private employers also could be recipients of such grants under such a program if they operate in ways consistent with the above sustainability agenda. Such interventions would help fashion a more politically effective citizenry that, reflexively, would ensure that the state become even more democratic. They would also build their own constituency while easing pressures on the environment and on individuals.

Assuring these opportunities for all opens up the possibility of democratizing workplaces in ways that might advance greater racial and gender equality within them. Jobs, child allowances, and adequate care for the elderly would help us place a higher value on nurturing and protecting the vulnerable. This would repay society by easing the burdens of nurturers, as well as by devoting more time and resources to the upbringing of children. For the poorest citizens, an adequate job provides an opportunity to enter consumer society, to purchase housing, transportation options, and access to the media needed to be full participants.

Unlike other full employment programs, not all the new jobs would come from production of endlessly more goods. When workers have more chance to determine their own hours of work, as productivity grows, many will choose to work fewer hours and thereby open up jobs for others (Schor, 1991). In addition, more democratic workplaces and more time for family and self-development can lead many to distinguish between endless material growth unreflectively accepted as an imperative and growth defined by the choices of freer political and economic actors. Finally, the imperative of growth and the fear of scarcity have played a crucial role in fostering the zero-sum character of contemporary civilization and the disciplines it imposes.

Interconnections

Nothing better illustrates the need for a multilevel approach to our dilemmas than our continued reliance on oil for domestic energy and transportation. In one way or another, the automobile is implicated in many of our most pressing social and ecological problems. The very centrality of the auto in our economy and culture is often cited as the reason why Americans are unlikely to make the sacrifices needed to effect a sustainable economy.

Alternatives to a transportation system dependent on individual gas-powered vehicles could, if implemented in appropriate ways, receive widespread support. Part of the process of building such support is the recognition of the auto's role in our economy. The importation of foreign oil is a large part of our balance of trade deficit. Auto exhaust is implicated in both ozone and greenhouse effect problems. In a more immediate sense, the auto is the primary cause of significant levels of smog, implicated in a range of health problems in major urban areas (Dockery et al., 1993). In addition, the auto has very burdensome economic implications for individuals. Americans already spend one out of every five dollars on the auto—its care and feeding—and they spend ever more time in their cars. Experts expect average commuting time to show a steady increase (Yago, 1986). As more families are compelled—in large measure by the economic demands fostered by the evolution of our system—to have two breadwinners, total adult time spent in the auto will grow further. With that time, the costs associated with auto ownership will continue to rise.

Despite these considerations, the emphasis on conservation, relatively well developed in the late 1970s and early 1980s, has nearly halted. From renewed advertising of gasoline as a source of power to emphasis on the auto and open travel and even to some moves to larger cars on the part of auto makers, we have seen a definite lessening of the conservation initiative.

This suggests that oil prices are too central a matter to be left simply to the market. Time horizons are too long for adequate market response to rapid increases in domestic oil and gas prices. Even the Reagan administration partially recognized this fact in its continued adherence to and development of the domestic petroleum reserve. More effective than this initiative, however, would be regulation of the price of oil through a gradually escalating tax on oil (Alperovitz & Faux, 1984). This approach would keep that price moving upward gently, regardless of the world price. The funds generated by such taxation would be distributed to individual taxpayers in the form of rebates so that the poor would not be especially disadvantaged by this approach. In addition, funds raised by this program could be used to supplement existing mass transit programs. The efficacy of such an approach could also be supplemented by a program that Amory Lovins suggests, that of "feebates" (1995). Because the most important decision individuals make with regard to fuel economy is at the time of vehicle purchase, Lovins argues for high taxes on new gas guzzlers and feebates, or rebates, to purchasers of high-mileage cars.

Greater subsidization of mass transit combined with greater economic incentives to make use of it could lead to dramatic increases in ridership and a greater public interest in it. In dealing with the political resistance such subsidization inevitably elicits, citizens must be made aware of the level of both explicit and implicit subsidy already enjoyed by the private auto—from road construction to the military budget.[2] Citizen acceptance of public transit alternatives could be facilitated by further efforts to integrate bus, subway, and rail service with the auto through park-and-ride and corridor bus lanes. Given a several-generation commitment to the auto and patterns of suburbanization built on it, the only feasible alternatives are ones that strive to integrate the auto with more efficient forms of travel by reducing congestion, traffic time, and commuter frustration.

Transit decision makers must also become more accountable. Since the Progressive era, one major goal of so-called reformers has been to make mass transit policy the prerogative of appointed but independent state and regional agencies. Consequently, there has been little opportunity for average working-class citizens to participate effectively in transit decisions; these citizens also have experienced considerable anger at the decisions made.

Funds need to be made available to state and local authorities with the proviso that, in the language of Lyndon Johnson's poverty war, maximum feasible participation of citizenry be required. This means that broad transit policy would be made by democratically elected representatives. When implemented by transit boards, their rules would be arrived at through a public hearing process and their decision process would be open and accessible. In addition, economic incentives should be created to spur this process. Localities that make more than average gains in ridership and in decreases in the use of oil, as well as time spent in transit, should be rewarded with supplemental funds. Toward this end, incentives should be developed to preserve and extend opportunities for travel on bike paths, sidewalks, and the like so that transportation need not always rely on energy intensive means.

Mass transit by itself is no panacea. It could serve to replicate the inequities and environmental problems of suburban development, distributing the middle and upper-middle classes further into relatively undeveloped areas. In addition, suburban living along present lines is inconceivable without continued reliance on the auto. The affordability of housing; the availability, nature, and cost of transportation; and patterns of local economic development are all interrelated phenomena that have been at the heart of the economic and social dilemmas of modern times.

In this context, the role of residential and land use planning becomes important, including greater use by states and localities of cluster zoning. At a minimum, states and localities need to initiate so-called cluster zoning ordinances. By requiring developers to preserve some open space, clustered housing saves on road construction and sewage and water costs within new developments and helps ease urban sprawl. It also provides a better context for the development of more rational transit options. The difficulty of developing concrete options is clear in the case of zoning. On the one hand, people want to preserve the environment. On the other, there is popular resistance to using zoning for environmental objectives. Sometimes the options we choose can address legitimate fears, for example, loss of value for private homes that were bought under other value assumptions.[3] Environmentalists should strive to make home ownership secure, for example, by proposing municipal insurance funds for residential housing. We have in mind a program that would protect the purchase price of homes up to a reasonable middle-class standard. Values would be adjusted for inflation; owners would be compensated against loss of value resulting from zoning or other environmental regulations. In the process of such debates, however, environmentalists also need to make clear the ways that unregulated development can undermine property values and foster economically costly transportation problems.

Another policy option would be a low-interest loan fund that would make available funds to urban and rural communities that meet the following criteria: a mix of housing cost options, preservation of substantial open space, and plans to integrate, through transportation and land use policies, the business, retail, and residential aspects of the community (Hayden, 1984). A low-interest program of this sort, especially if it were accompanied by a program to replace the tax deduction with a tax credit,[4] would pump a great deal more money into low- and moderate-income housing. If properly constructed, this program could mitigate racial, gender, and ethnic inequalities. With home prices difficult to afford even for most middle-class citizens, this federal program might have a chance to gain a substantial constituency.

Historically, local governments have been reluctant to play more than a minimal role in land use planning out of fear that objectives would deter all development and thus undermine the local economy. Land use planning can be more easily defended and advanced when states and municipalities play a larger role in economic development in general.

State governments already have considerable economic resources in the form of pension funds. Some of these could be used to pump money into local housing markets to provide loans and equity capital for local businesses in such areas as recycling key resources, local processing and distribution of local and regional foods. The use of pension funds in this fashion is one way to encourage the grassroots economic development of the sort Hawken (1993) advocates but does not provide tangible support for (Gunn & Gunn, 1991).

For example, loans for housing construction could be contingent on contracting, to some reasonable degree, with local producers of recycled materials and other locally produced products. Pensions are intended to protect the economic security of the recipients; no one denies that return on investment is crucial. Unacknowledged is the importance of the economic viability of the local economy and, thereby, the community's stability.

No state can control its full economic destiny. Shifts in the larger economy cause economic declines; economic development itself is often uneven. Uneven economic development causes forced relocation and blunts many citizens' interests in preservation of the immediate environment. States by themselves have neither sufficient resources nor the political and legal capacity to combat these problems. Thus, economic development will still require an important federal component. For example, federal housing programs, or programs of infrastructure repair, could target some money for declining communities.

Energy policy is critical to a sustainability program; many sound proposals have been made and some good programs have been tried. For example, the restoration of tax credits for conservation and solar energy is clearly called for. Tax incentives and utility regulation to encourage the development of decentralized, cogeneration alternatives to conventional energy and heat sources have the most potential for gain. When tax incentives take the form of credits capped at a reasonable maximum, they can be cost-effective. Policy must ensure that public funds do not go to those who are able and likely to make the changes anyway. When proposals such as these are supplemented with efforts to enhance the home owner's ability to assess their worth and participate in their implementation, we can expect them to be administered more efficiently and to be more effective. The more effective they are, the more energy transition jobs they will produce.

These ideas are meant to suggest some parameters of a sustainability agenda that would emphasize the deployment of clean technologies rather than the control of pollution caused by "dirty" ones. Sustainable technologies have several related features: They entail less environmental risk and they limit inequities and hidden risks associated with environmental cost displacements; they minimize the use of nonrenewable resources; and they can be made economically competitive or even advantageous within a relatively short time frame (see Goodstein, 1995). They also are user friendly; this fact alone is of environmental and political importance. The consumer can learn to deploy such technologies in home or workplace relatively easily; his or her ability to do so improves their viability (Strange, 1988). Greater citizen knowledge and control can build a constituency for alternative technologies.

Their use can lessen the frustration associated with dependence on anonymous utility companies and allow consumers to become an effective check against excessive costs and unresponsive or improper administration. Finally, although some important standards and incentives will be defined nationally, the structure of these proposals requires substantial local decision making.

Further consideration of the need for an ecological "industrial policy" is warranted to speed the development of such technologies, partly by offsetting the artificial market power now enjoyed by established industries and utilities employing unsustainable production processes and energy use. Barry Commoner (1990) recognizes this need by calling for government purchase of alternative vehicles to speed achievement of economies of scale and competitive viability of alternatives to petrochemicals. In his view, democratically arrived at choices such as these would create economic activity and more effectively wed concerns about the environment with economic security. Such policies would break the perceived trade-off, popularized in the media, between environmental safety and jobs. The need for federal and state involvement is even greater in the case of petrochemical products used in agriculture and industry. Here a clear environmental case for phaseout can be made, but research priorities focus on, and have even discouraged, the development of alternatives (see Strange, 1988, for a discussion of the ways petrochemical and agribusiness interests have shaped university research priorities).

However much we may wish to meet environmental needs at the level of the community, state, or region, we cannot escape a central federal role. A federal role is essential for two reasons. First, only the federal government has the resources and legal muscle to offset the unfair, unecological, and uneconomic institutional advantages unsustainable industries now depend on. Second, the federal government is the only forum where citizens come together as a nation to define and redefine how we want to live together. Making such a case, however, requires addressing contemporary concerns about big government (see Chapter 3 in this volume).

These concerns are familiar. Government cannot correctly pick "winners" because it inevitably plays favorites based on political considerations. Government regulations are ineffective and, by reducing competition, lessen economic efficiency. And the federal government limits our freedoms.

The sustainability principles, objectives, rights, and suggestions we offer here are designed to answer these concerns in two ways. First, they increase the ability to effect the process in design and implementation stages by citizens—as consumers, as employees, as unfairly disadvantaged property owners and business people, and as voters. For example, government today is measured by its inability to regulate effectively and judiciously, with little consideration given to the serious constraints it operates under (see Chapter 2 in this volume). Second, a reconsideration of the role of the federal government is necessitated by the need to offset inefficient and unecological advantages now enjoyed by institutions that unfairly dominate relevant markets. Consider that our present economic institutions already pick winners, but these are somewhat less efficient, and greatly less sustainable, than they would be if their operations put less constraints on the rest of us and were guided by the proposals we offer. All levels of government can and should be partners in a sustainability agenda. As our political system is presently structured, the federal government alone has the leverage to do so most effectively.

Yet government has made serious mistakes. If the federal role remains important, it is incumbent on us to make it work as effectively and in as little onerous a manner as possible.

Reforming Government as We Know It

Consider the case of government subsidies. The form that such subsidies should take is important not only to the results achieved but also to public reception of the policies. Priority should be given to the forms of basic and applied research and technology development essential to sustainability but unlikely to be undertaken by the private sector. These could be undertaken through joint public-private partnerships between firms in an industry and public universities or other government agencies. Perhaps the most obvious need today is in the area of alternatives to the gasoline-powered car and in basic energy research.

Basic and applied research has always been a priority for the U.S. government, though it has usually been undertaken under the auspices of the military. Today it is essential that the public interest in sustainability guide that effort. It is crucial, however, that such policies not follow the Pentagon model in one regard. They must not become an endless gravy train for the private sector. Eban Goodstein (1995) suggests that policies should place a time limit on the years that research subsidies are available. Under such an approach, corporations would be able to develop new alternatives, but would have an incentive to market them in a timely manner within a competitive environment.

Government can foster clean technologies in a cost-effective manner. Neoclassical concepts of marginal price and marginal benefit can play a key role here, whatever the level of protection we are trying to achieve. Thus, if one is interested in using tax policy to encourage alternative fuels to reduce ground-level ozone, it may make sense to ask whether the marginal gain from an increase in taxes on fuel and cars in Utah is equal to the marginal gain a similar increase would foster in New Jersey. Greater benefits may accrue from relatively more taxes (and compensatory rebates) in certain areas than others.

Any policy instrument will be blunt, subject to mistakes based on reasonable but incorrect guesses as to pollution patterns, cost curves, consumer response. Only by following data on particular pollution problems and productivity patterns in various sectors can these instruments be adjusted. Furthermore, public knowledge and concern may be needed to discipline government's (or business's) work. Toward this end, there is no substitute for broad public access to information about investment levels and productivity changes, environmental dangers, and the results of government policies.

For years, we have had a soil conservation service that has helped the farmer understand modern farming, with both negative and positive results. Today we need an energy conservation service. A conservation service would make available at the local level advice from nonprofit and governmental agencies about energy-saving techniques. Such a service, especially if combined with the provision of tools on a community basis, a renewed emphasis on products that can be understood and repaired at the household level, and more free time (discussed below), would make us less rather than more burdened and hassled. More broadly, an adequate science and technology policy would provide a broad range of expertise to municipal and nonprofit organizations (Dickson, 1984). These groups would then be better able to assess the claims of federal and corporate experts as to the propriety of certain new technologies.

Requirements as to kinds of packaging and reuse and recycling of certain resources facilitate much less destructive forms of consumption. They can be combined with demands by consumers both individually and collectively for forms of products that consumers themselves or within their neighborhoods can remake and redesign to meet individual needs and desires. This process of breaking down some of the barriers between production and consumption can improve both processes. It would allow citizens to demand, control, and sometimes even to fashion products that more efficiently meet certain needs and thus to limit the consumption imperative implicit in the current way of doing business.

Redeeming government will, however, require more than simply a change in policy. Several elements of our general policy, such as our suggestions on transit, would have to be implemented by bureaucracies at state and federal levels. State and local agencies would have to implement policies regarding appropriate housing and development planning. How do we keep bureaucracies accountable and how do we ensure that they perform their tasks fairly and efficiently? We might even consider including enterprise zones, but only ones based on charters of corporate responsibility to include such features as: keeping substantial capital generated in the neighborhood, fair labor standards, worker education and empowerment for self-development.

Wholesale privatization of these functions is no answer to the problems that currently beset the public sector. There are good reasons to hire private contractors to paint the local prison. Running prisons, guarding prisoners, and establishing adequate rehabilitation programs are, however, another matter. In one case, criteria for a good job are reasonably clear, firms routinely provide such work to private sector purchasers, and the broad functioning of the society is not at stake. There are many policy and implementation tasks, from schools to toxic tests to public health activities to maintenance of scenic and recreational areas, that may be better left in the public sector. The alternative is an increased probability of diminished or even dangerous provision of services necessary to the maintenance of a civilized society.

These considerations are not intended to suggest that there is no need for reform within the public sector. Nevertheless, many of the problems with public sector performance have to do with the relations between the law making and law enforcement branches of government on the one hand and the private economy on the other hand. This is a complex triadic relationship in need of reform. There is considerable slippage between expression of congressional intent in such areas as toxic regulations and the actual performance in rule making and application. But can we simply blame bureaucracy for these failings? Because private investment is the primary way to create jobs and foster social equity, an elected Congress has an interest in going on record as in favor of relatively strict health standards but not pushing these to the point where private capital will no longer make the investments needed to sustain economic development.

In such a context, it is easy for Congress to pass broad and generally well-intentioned laws and to allow bureaucracies the task of implementing these in such a way that does not destroy jobs. When jobs are lost, the bureaucracy and its inefficiencies are routinely cited. Not surprisingly, bureaucrats are sent mixed messages. Relatively lax oversight, poor pay by market standards of even top level administrators, and a willingness to allow these bureaucrats to circulate between the private and public sectors all add to the mixed message.

An environmental agenda geared toward full employment and alternative technologies would address part of this problem. It would lessen some of the regulatory burdens associated with detailed toxicology assessment and prioritization of relatively dangerous substances. An approach to both toxics and inequalities that emphasizes social goods and greater worker empowerment at the point of production would lift some economic and regulatory burdens off bureaucracy and free it to pursue its goals in a more thorough way. Bureaucratic experts could set more general assessment standards and serve as an important source of research and information.

Bureaucracy's internal structure is not immune from problems, however. Some critics of bureaucracy and interest group liberalism have argued in favor of limiting public access to the bureaucracy on the grounds that its responsibility is simply to enforce law, not to make it. We believe, however, that this distinction can never be as precise as in textbooks and that Congress must give public bureaucracy some discretion. In such a context, the bureaucratic process should be as open as possible and the public, through democratic channels, needs to assert a public interest.

Public bureaucracies are in need of clearer guidance in terms of both the laws they are to enforce and the indicators they are to use to assess goal attainment. Regular legislative oversight of goal attainment, including broad public testimony as to the efficacy of law and its enforcement, must be part of the process. Better internal incentives could be established by making public service, especially the more important technical and administrative functions, attractive careers and by further limiting the "revolving door" in the public sector.

The organization of the work process itself within bureaucracy must also receive closer scrutiny. Public service is not inherently inefficient. Much of the demoralization and inefficiency of the public sector springs from its easy adoption of the worst forms of private sector workplace organization. The modern bureaucracy assigns supervisors inordinate control, but in the process, it deprives workers of the knowledge and incentives to perform an adequate job. As public servants are treated with more esteem, their professional self-esteem and commitment will grow.

Reforms of public sector work organization have occurred in a few cities and states and are worthy of further examination. New York City has greatly reduced the cost of vehicle maintenance by giving front-line employees the training and opportunities to maintain their own repair (Lynch & Markusen, 1994). Such efforts need to be broadened to give employees more input into the overall agency process, including a voice in the selection of professional supervisors. Part of such an effort should be the development of career tracks and incentive systems internal to the structure that are based on individual or group contributions to the goals of the particular agency. Better guidance for administrative agencies, establishment of goal attainment measures and incentive systems based on goal attainment, and broader worker input into workplace organization could change not only agency performance but also public perceptions and willingness to fund such performance.

Finally, adequate environmental, transit, and industrial policies require a citizenry informed about such issues with the willingness and ability to insist on adequate oversight of the entire process. Many of the reforms sketched above address these concerns. Full employment provides a modicum of present security needed to pursue environmental issues whose implications relate to long-term concerns. People with more direct experience in housing, transit, products, the environment, and other diverse activities and with the time for more rounded development are more likely to take an active interest in and have more knowledge of the ways bureaucracy can facilitate citizen initiatives.

Progress along each line helps facilitate progress along others. Hours reduction can facilitate political participation, one purpose of which is to fashion common solutions to pressing social and environmental problems. Social goods, those facilities and amenities, such as public parks and public recreational areas, that benefit most of us if provided by anyone, are most likely to be funded adequately by the public when inordinate inequalities have been reduced and citizens are more willing and able to seek common solutions. Provision of social goods helps create jobs, reduce inequality, and in turn foster a great social commitment to the public provision of those services that reduce the economic and time constraints on all. To the extent such a political dialectic unfolds in the North, it takes pressure off the demand for those scarce raw materials now desperately needed for development in the South. Enabling this process to unfold would, however, entail some changes within the modern workplace.

The World of Work

More interesting, less onerously supervised work has important social and ecological consequences. It enables work to become more of a craft and somewhat more satisfying. Although managerial hierarchy and authority will always be necessary—expertise will always be differential, all of us need some stick as well as some carrots—freeing us from unnecessary hierarchy and artificial authority also helps mitigate the compulsion to status climb through work. C. Wright Mills (discussed in DeLuca, 1995) criticized the trade unions of his day for exemplifying the pure form of alienation, wanting less and less work for more and more money. In today's world, working less no longer seems a realistic option. Yet there is still a desire for more leisure, which itself can put our work lives in the proper perspective, one that has important environmental benefits. If work is fairly compensated but also has rewards other than money, if more leisure becomes a realistic choice, the cycle of work and spend—working harder so one can spend more—can be eased, and with it the imperative of unsustainable economic growth. To the extent that ecologists wish to speed the transition to more sustainable development, they need to think about the ways in which the organization of work itself creates ambivalence about, if not resistance to, their goals.

Work that becomes more of a craft has other environmental benefits. If we reject the contention that knowledge of ecology can be clear, unambiguous, and incontestable, we cannot assume that alternative technologies and products will not carry potential risks to the health of humans and other animals. Because the workplace is an important locus of technological problems and workers are often the first victims, employees with greater knowledge and control over technology use and choice can be a first line of defense for society against dangerous technologies or socially destructive technological change.

The benefits of broader worker participation also go beyond such traditional economic questions as productivity enhancement (see Chapter 3 in this volume). When people develop more skills and confidence on the job, these carry over into problem solving, including the ability to participate effectively in voluntary community organizations and to hold elected officials, bureaucrats, and business people accountable.

A more participatory workplace can be achieved in ways that do not involve micromanagement by government. Changes in pension fund policy would give unions and municipalities the right to use their own savings as incentives to businesses to create more productive and fairer workplaces. Participation in research consortia should be contingent on employers' commitment to expand workers' opportunities to participate in broader corporate policy regarding the design and marketing of products, the establishment of job ladders, and the long-term financial management of the company. It is not government's task to impose one model of workplace organization, but it can use this carrot to leverage an active and independent voice for workers in the process of corporate reorganization. Other related reforms would also facilitate this process.

Fairer workplaces do not create equality, but they limit the extent of unnecessary inequalities in socially and ecologically beneficial ways. The right to an opportunity to work and the right to organize workplaces more productively are not and should not be the same as the right to identical and identically compensated careers. There is no and can be no such right. It means only a reasonable level of security as one seeks to fashion a career rewarded by effort, experience, and skill. Historically, there have been a few U.S. and many European examples of workplaces where employees collaborated in corporate planning and had varying degrees of responsibility for design of the work process itself. Movement along these lines lessens both the need for and the possibility of creating excessive layers of supervision. It also reduces the likelihood of fostering status distinctions between workers that are more disempowering than economic. In workplaces organized along these lines, skills tend to be more widely dispersed and income disparities less severe. Those forms of invidious consumption, through which one demonstrates one has "the right stuff" or is part of the right group to exercise leadership, are less likely in a context of broad skill development and worker input into corporate policy and the choice of management personnel. Such an agenda builds more cooperation within the workplace and fosters greater willingness to pursue a politics of social goods in the public arena. Reforms along these lines can, in short, lift some pressures off both human beings and the environment.

Greater employee voice in the question of the length of their working hours is important on both social and ecological grounds. If more productive employees could take their productivity dividends in the form of more free time rather than more wages, some of the impetus toward unnecessary consumption could be slowed. Having attained the economic basis for a good quality of life, people could choose to extend their leisure, to enhance their contributions to their communities, or to spend more time with their families and friends. The choice would be theirs. Government need not and should not micromanage this change. Through legislative action, however, it can outlaw forced overtime and define as an unfair labor practice employer unwillingness in collective bargaining to offer compensation for productivity increases in the form of shorter hours (Schor, 1991). These changes would level the playing field without dictating what employers and employees decide. Indeed, many would undoubtedly choose to keep working and spending; for those with less economic security, we would endorse this choice.

The International Context

Liberal theory has long regarded society as sustained by the territorial state. Government represents, in liberal thought, a fusion of geography and history and is seen as the proper repository for programs and initiatives needed to sustain the market and family. The internationalization of the market, goods, services, and technology choices profoundly challenges the traditional liberal view. Indeed, for a sustainability agenda it creates a paradox. We need the nation state to provide the political boundaries within which we can improve the quality of our lives yet we need to go beyond it to make our efforts as successful and humane as possible. We need, in short, to ensure that standards similar in nature, although not identical in detail or scope, to the ones suggested here become requirements of all nations. Otherwise, assuming the agenda we have suggested is adopted, three tendencies will emerge. First, we will witness massive capital flight. Second, we will restrict trade and capital flight in ways that will hurt less developed nations while angering more powerful, developed ones and making our own economy less efficient and productive. Third, we will make war more likely. All these tensions will weaken our will to hold onto our own sustainability program.

There is no simple way to break free of this paradox, but there are demanding ways through international negotiation, political activism, and, when necessary, sanctions. Such standards are not detrimental to Third World development. Quite the contrary, they can also give other states the incentives and economic resources on which to premise future sustainable patterns of development. If trade agreements ensure that domestic labor everywhere is compensated in proportion to its real productivity, trade can then help foster the consumer and tax base on which indigenous development can proceed.

This does not mean that identical wage standards should be imposed on all nations. It does imply, however, that wage standards in trade agreements need to be pegged to the average level of productivity in each nation. When firms make decisions as to where to locate in today's unregulated market, net labor costs are a large factor. If industrial labor in Mexico is 80% as productive as that in the United States but receives 10% of the wage, more and more industrial labor will be carried out in Mexico. Wage standards set at 80% of U.S. norms would deter capital movement based solely on oppressive labor practices in Mexico. But they would not deter all trade and would foster higher wages on both sides of the border. Higher wages and smoother development—especially for so-called Third World states—can provide nations with the capital for needed social and environmental improvements. As long as the corporate employer is able to use capital mobility as a means of extracting monopoly profits, these nations will never be able to recoup the resources for development of an adequate social infrastructure.

Adequate labor and environmental standards negotiated across borders can be composed as win-win formulas for citizens of developing and developed nations alike. Programs of technology assistance that encourage development of renewable energy and sustainable transit in developing nations not only benefit them but also lessen global environmental problems while easing resource depletion and prices. Upgrading employee empowerment abroad mitigates capital flight that currently hurts workers in industrialized nations. By fostering more egalitarian and ecological patterns of development in these societies, we would help developing nations avoid dangerous and unfair paths of industrial development.

Achievement of these ambitious goals will not be easy. World government is neither feasible nor desirable. Although negotiations between governments are essential, meeting these goals will require active engagement of citizens, both pushing their governments on them, and collaborating across borders with each other to attain them.

Despite the win-win possibilities in such negotiations, such a process is not without its perils. When basic democratic, environmental, economic, or fairness values are repeatedly violated, we shall have to draw the line. We shall also have to be alert to cases in which cultural differences that enforce discrimination by gender, race, ethnicity, or religion effectively give their elites an unfair advantage in attracting capital, further disenfranchising the exploited groups. We must, however, always be sensitive that we do not—and do not let our government or our own elites—convert all forms of difference into enmity, but rather attempt to broaden, as far as is consistent with justice, the sphere for constructive negotiation.

Specificity Within Universalism

Just as rigid politics based on difference will undermine sustainability efforts abroad, so too will it do the same at home. Indeed, these are often indissolubly linked. We therefore also need to address the origins and legacy of domestic identity politics. Racism and sexism can be reduced through a broad-based politics of universal economic empowerment. But they have also a resilience, independent of socioeconomic status, forged in our history that must be considered separately.

Although we have argued that universal programs are essential for sustainable and equitable policies, equity requires consideration of the anxieties inside racial and gender hierarchies and the exclusionary practices they foster. Take the example of social security. Social security is one of the premiere American social policies based on universal principles. In fact, even here, the politics of race and gender played a crucial role in the evolution of social security legislation. Franklin Roosevelt's decision to exclude seasonal and domestic workers from the original old-age program and his devolution of so much responsibility to the states for unemployment insurance and welfare reflected his unwillingness to challenge the highly racialized Southern labor system and the Southern Democrats on whom he relied (Gordon, 1994). Roosevelt's concession itself had a history.

From the earliest days of our nation, the racialization of differences has been essential to our social structure even as it was built upon the legacies of the lands from which some of us came. Indeed, race and gender have always been essential to the complex formation of identities. A group of refugees from Europe's religious wars saw themselves as God's chosen people. Fearful of death and living in a turbulent world, they sought to establish their distinctiveness both from the native peoples and from medieval traditions. They regarded their ability to transform nature as proof of their excellence in God's eyes. To buttress their claim and to ease their own anxieties about their goals and their purposes, white men strove to distinguish themselves from women, who were viewed as limited by the exigencies of child rearing, and the more collectivist and "steady state" native societies on whom they in fact depended for many goods (Campbell, 1992).

This hierarchy was grounded on perceived physical differences, which were sketched and catalogued to buttress such a scheme. Though drawing exact racial and gender distinctions often proved difficult, the difficulties of and preconceptions brought to the process could be more easily evaded due to the empiricism of its practitioners. That empiricism refused to examine any possible role that cultural presuppositions would have in the construction of "natural" difference. "Hard cases" could thus become not occasions to question the categories or their origin but to demand further efforts to fit everyone in "his or her" place (Connolly, 1987). Such empiricism itself also encouraged a picture of nature as fully understandable and manipulable by men, who stood above it; and it further reinforced stereotypes about those who appeared to take a less instrumental orientation to the natural world, such as women and Native Americans. Elements of this picture thus reinforced each other in an ever-tightening circle, which was used to provide legitimacy to the whole ontology. Such ontologies reflexively created hostility in the "other," confirming in the dominant group the "natural" status of the subordinate peoples.

As we pointed out in our discussion of other influential sustainability agendas, the forms that racism and sexism have taken over time are not invariant. Racism and sexism once took the form of legal exclusion. In an era of formal legal equality, both are more often manifested through institutional policies and practices. These can include restrictions on the geographic areas to which loans are given to people, glass ceilings in careers, unnecessary educational or skill requirements for jobs, or the "savage inequalities" between schools in affluent neighborhoods and those in poor and minority ones (Kozol, 1991). They can also derive from performances on tests whose problematic premises go unquestioned but whose use "naturalizes" past deprivations by implying that the bell curves discovered are normal (Hernstein & Murray, 1994). In many instances, these practices are not outcomes of conscious racism or sexism, but they systematically damage self-esteem and life chances all the same.

Universal policies to promote a higher quality of life, including greater free time, more employment security, and effective workplace participation, could create a context in which it would be far easier to address these issues. They would also make it easier to address much of the anger of many working-class and middle-class white males toward government, women, minorities, and the poor. Where wages are stagnant and employment seems less secure, where work fails to tap one's abilities and is closely micromanaged, and where the workday seems to be without end, one plausible identity is to see oneself as earning enough to escape or to make it possible for one's children to do so. Welfare state policies that provide assistance to minorities or the poor challenge an identity about which many already harbor doubts. These policies deepen racial resentment by appearing to demean people's sacrifices.

Forms of politics that seek to solve problems of racial or gender exclusion solely through focus on affirmative action inevitably place an inordinate burden for change on working-class and lower managerial white males. From these workers' perspectives, these politics place the whole burden of America's racial and gender history squarely on their shoulders. Politics defined in this way is a recipe for further defensiveness and more exclusive identities. It undermines a politics of sustainability and real equity.

Affirmative action is far from alone in fostering wedge issues that divide constituencies having more in common than either may care to acknowledge. Nonetheless, it does pose some of the toughest questions of how to achieve equity in a world that is not likely to change soon. There are other histories of disadvantage. Although these disadvantages are clearly not as severe as those of African Americans or women, many white males have been disadvantaged by a combination of socioeconomic status and ethnic heritage. Still, from the point of view of those most historically disadvantaged, it is understandable why for them affirmative action today appears far more realistic—in spite of its political liabilities—than the color-blind society that was promised 30 years ago.

These real issues need full, open deliberation. In this regard, we take seriously the argument about affirmative action made by Joanne Barkan (1995). Indeed, her argument contains principles of equity that could have even broader application. Barkan argues persuasively that we need to "drop the defensiveness about scrutinizing individual programs. Affirmative action begs for democratic management, for careful design and monitoring by the people who live with it" (p. 463). Furthermore, "when a fair evaluation shows a program to be ineffective, fraud-ridden, wasteful, or unjust," we should "endorse revamping or dropping it" (p. 463).

When not subject to appraisal and deliberation, specially targeted programs may even run the risk of naturalizing and sedimenting the racial thinking they are designed to challenge. From this perspective, examination of the racial and gender practices within specific occupational fields, educational networks, and regions becomes appropriate. In some instances, application of basic nondiscrimination laws will be sufficient, whereas in other areas, where qualified citizens of particular backgrounds are disproportionately denied entry, more proactive strategies will be necessary. Even in these cases, however, at some point a sufficient beachhead may be achieved that such proactive strategies would no longer be necessary or appropriate. Determination of that point will be a contentious process, but it could be eased by greater recognition of both our past legacies of race and gender and their present reality and the ontological and political risks entailed by remedies that focus exclusively on race and gender.

In any case, there will be no easy way out. Acrimony exists today and, in racial matters, seems to be increasing. Oppressive racial, ethnic, and gender categorizations will be with us into the foreseeable future. Universal programs can ease these divisions, but they will not eliminate them. The very process of identity formation may always run the risk of producing "others." One may nonetheless hope for and strive to foster a politics that encourages each self at risk of naturalizing its own identity (and thereby demonizing the other) to recognize and combat that tendency in itself and thereby create an opening where it can discourage that tendency in others.

A Commons of Everyday Life

No political program or environmental or economic development policy is risk free. Indeed, one of the objectives of our analysis and proposals is to make knowledge of the benefits and risks and the potential for freedom and the added responsibilities they entail as accessible as possible to all interested citizens. At its most fundamental level, therefore, our objectives are democratic objectives—even when greater democracy may mean less environmentally sustainable choices. We think, however, that sufficient political space and environmental time exist today for us to resolve our most pressing environmental problems. Resolution is most likely, in our judgment, to the degree that Americans democratically participate in finding ways to improve the overall quality of life. In addition, to the degree we are involved in this process, we become more responsible for—and more committed to—the solutions we find. Environmental sustainability becomes politically sustainable.

A program that (1) provides secure jobs, (2) gives citizens opportunities to tap expertise and hold experts accountable and gain greater knowledge themselves, and (3) allows citizens to consider environmental and equity issues with their peers puts them in a position to choose the risks they are willing to incur for the quality of life they desire. A constituency with access to its own scientists and more broadly occupied with its own creative problem solving can better assess the demands made by government and industry. It will then more willingly accept truly unavoidable risks for the sake of generally recognized and widely distributed benefits.

We might call such an arrangement a *commons of everyday life*. The relation of this commons to the world of commodity production, government, and expertise will not be easy or automatic. Self-reliance carried to an extreme threatens not only the economic efficiencies that specialization has brought but even the development of human knowledge in a systematic way. Forms of individual production, just like commodity production, can be a threat to the natural and social worlds. We share with Ivan Illich (1978) the conviction that the balance between what we do for ourselves and in close, nonmarket collaboration with our friends and what is done for us has shifted too far in the latter direction. Unlike Illich, however, we do not assume that a firm boundary can be established marking a territory we call self-sufficient and personally rewarding homesteads and neighborly cooperation.

Indeed, the very process of boundary setting is itself an integral part of democratic deliberation, and we too must establish some markers. Still, discussion and elaboration of common discontents can help develop a new-found confidence in one's ability to articulate grievances and seek change, which itself makes participation less intimidating and more likely. For example, Andrew Szasz (1994) describes the ways in which community mobilization against toxic disposal facilities, often seen as the prototypically parochial defensive activity known as NIMBY, changed the lives of the participants. He remarks of interviews with these activists, many of whom were full-time mothers whose initial focus was primarily only on immediate family issues:

> The process of participation changed them in every way. It transformed their understanding of the world. It changed their self-image and in effect totally changed how they defined their lives. Disillusioned and angered by their experiences . . . their new political understandings, their anger, or their deeply felt ethic of responsibility made them, however reluctantly, accept the role of "activist." They have become public persons. In that process they . . . have become more confident, more skilled. (p. 154)

Such a process is far from automatic and is not without its risks and downsides. Nor is the political organization and mobilization that will be necessary to gain wider purchase for quality of life concerns at all easy to come by. Still, within contemporary culture, the experience of lack of time for friends, family, and community endeavors, or the way in which working harder never seems to get one far enough, are often felt as a private trouble or, alternately, as one of the natural features of modern life that one can do little about. Many often view environmental problems as serious but beyond effective control. To the degree that opportunities to deliberate and participate can mitigate such personalism and fatalism, we may find ourselves with more room for individuality even as we spend more energy solving common problems. The more knowledge, confidence, and inner strengths we have, the more we can protect ourselves from onerous forms of politics.

This approach suggests the creation of time, space, tools, and cultural and educational resources so that individuals can achieve greater self-reliance, though not literal self-sufficiency. For example, it also means that in the area of energy conservation, we must recognize the vital role of the consumer. Long-term energy savings depend not simply on the importation by the owner of some exotic or even "soft path" technology, such as photovoltaics, but on the understanding by him or her of how these technologies fit within the home.[5]

Our overall approach does not imply that everyone will wish to or can do everything. Rather, individuals should have greater opportunity outside of work to develop other skills through which they can meet needs and advance interests. The very development of the broader understandings and skills is not only instrumental, however. It is a good in itself. The development of an intrinsic interest in such knowledge and skills is one answer to dependence on commodities for identity formation or professionally controlled forms of expertise for our well-being. There is considerable evidence that such interest exists, in fact, that its frustration is perceived as an emerging issue in our society (Schor, 1991).

An ecological approach to sustainable development and to appropriate technologies asks us to place a high premium on the significance of human work and human skills. It implies that the hope of many, across the ideological spectrum, that benign automation can itself solve our problems is partly illusory. It suggests that compulsive efforts to displace all work and skills by technology both create dangers we are ill equipped to handle and rob humans of an important source of purpose. This perspective itself has an additional implication: Some downscaling of productive enterprises and adjustment of the design of technologies are necessary to enable us as independent beings to meet our own needs, as well as those of the community. Even a technological revolution crafted with the best intentions is no guarantor of greater human freedom.

The argument here can be interpreted as a form of teleology; indeed, some set of assumptions is always necessary. In our development of this notion—especially in our insistence on the central role of individuality and democracy—it is more a light teleology (one we return to in the next chapter) rather than one claiming to embrace all aspects of the human personality. The direction within the self that we point to is just one of many. We do suggest, however, that there is some proclivity within human beings to seek productive activity and creativity. These can be motivated by the desire to serve wider human purposes than compensation, status, or respect. Sometimes these activities integrate body and mind while contributing to the sustenance of others. The more our work and leisure activities call for craft and the more we can answer that call, the more independent we become. To the extent we can develop some variety of skills and interests in informal settings with others who do also, that sense of independence grows.

There is also some proclivity—and need—to solve problems in common. For centuries, we have called this politics. The more confidence we have as citizens and the more we are politically equal citizens, the more independent we are. As our skills as consumers, employees, and citizens develop, the less dependent we are on others, whether distant suppliers of oil, managers in the firm, or politicians at the United Nations, in Washington, DC, or in city hall.

Notes

1. We discuss the reasons for resentment of white working class males confined to narrow and dead-end jobs who find government support of other disadvantaged groups as an affront to their identity in Chapter 3.

2. Studies have suggested that gasoline would have to be in the four-dollar-a-gallon range to reflect the implicit subsidy to the auto (Worldwatch Institute, 1989).

3. We do not endorse the Wise Use movement's claim that every loss of value due to environmental regulation must be compensated. Nevertheless, citizens do have well-founded concerns about the loss of their life savings as, for example, caused by changes in zoning laws.

4. A tax credit allows an individual to reduce the amount he or she pays the government by the amount of the credit. A deduction allows an individual to reduce the amount of income subject to taxation by the amount of the deduction. Because incomes are taxed at different marginal rates, the higher the tax bracket one is in, the greater the benefit derived from the deduction. In general, tax credits are a more egalitarian way to use the tax code to advance social goals than deductions.

5. Strange (1988) discusses the role that farmers can play in making solar drying systems more effective when those systems are designed to be user-friendly.

7 Conclusion
Sustainable Democracy

Democracy as a Resource

In the United States, we are fond of talking about institutional gridlock, but we think less about the systemic and personal binds we also experience. Indeed, these are related. As a society, we depend on material growth; as individuals, we employ consumption as a liberating strategy but we lament the inability of our lawmakers to solve environmental problems. Less often do we fully consider the array of constraints they too find themselves operating under. So we blame them.

As a people, we want more equity and fairness for ourselves; many of us would like these extended to historically disadvantaged people, but once again we find ourselves trapped. We question and fear—sometimes correctly—that advancing the position of others will undermine our own positions. Perhaps we can find a common program to aid all of us, but the self-identities we define generate their own politics of exclusivity—of race, ethnicity, gender, and status.

We also have nostalgia for a "lost" quality of life. Yet we have not really lost the hope that contemporary life can be made better, that as a people we can find a common path out of the dilemmas of our daily lives. For these hopes to become realized, we need to become better aware of the binds, constraints, and limitations imposed on us and that we impose on ourselves and on others. Each bind is a thread in a web of stasis. Pulling on only one thread runs the risk of focusing political attention away from the others, keeping us ensnared. If we remain entrapped in this way, we will prevent ourselves from developing the sense of common purpose and the common programs needed to advance the quality of our lives.

As we begin to see interconnections, a new sense of grounded optimism can develop. If our discontents have common threads, perhaps alternatives exist that we can turn to that can provide a realistic better way. If we cannot solve environmental problems within the present path of work and spend, perhaps there are ways we can redirect the road we travel.

Which direction is our future? That will depend, in part, on the kind of politics we countenance in the future. Awareness of the most important of these binds, as well as plausible ways to create opportunities for a better life, creates the possibility of more fruitful interventions. There are important rays of hope.

A widespread perception exists that, ecologically, we cannot go on as we are. Sometimes this is wedded to exaggerated pictures of doom and even to biocentric visions of nature, but most often it is grounded in a desire to live in an environmentally safe and sound world. Moreover, although we are sometimes a divided people, we are still a democratic people. We may not all understand this term in exactly the same way, but most of us are committed to free expression, even of those views we abhor, and we believe as political actors our votes should count equally. Democracy American style places a heavy premium on the right to deliberate, the dignity of the individual, and the hope that political disputes can be resolved democratically. These are important resources for discussing openly our discontents and hopes, for exploring the defensive identities and postures we sometimes adopt, and for getting beyond these to forge common solutions.

Politics that focuses on environmental problems and overall quality of life can find a place in contemporary discourse. Such politics are more likely to challenge both environmental dangers and social injustices if it encompasses respect and concern even for those against whom its supporters have defined their own identity. Listening in this way is also likely to improve the quality of politics.

To achieve sustainable economic development, therefore, we need another kind of sustainability. We call this *sustainable democracy*. We mean this in two senses. First, the problems we face are resilient, interconnected, and powerful. We have suggested throughout this work their breadth, from toxic waste in communities to global warming, from racial politics at home to fundamentalism and xenophobia in international affairs, from the systemic imperative of unreflective growth to the individual proclivity to spending beyond one's needs and means, from declining communities to the internationalization of the market. We have also suggested a general approach to their resolution, as well as specific ways to attack them. Most important, we have tried to indicate a way in which Americans can compose a repertoire of reforms that together provide a viable alternative framework—one that can generate a productive economy within a sound environment.

We believe this program is plausible enough to be embraced by a wide range of citizens. Indeed, we hope it addresses important interests of all citizens. Moreover, it has little chance of success in any but a political culture like ours, committed to democracy. Only the kind of support, pressure, and wisdom that can be generated from the top, bottom, and middle will bring it about. In this sense, only a fuller democracy of this sort is environmentally sustainable and will be able to address environmental problems in a way that is politically sustainable.

Second, sustainable democracy refers to more than the political viability of programs of action, or even the viability of the system as a whole. It also refers to an attitude about the openness of democratic deliberation and an awareness that even democracy itself entails risks and costs. However, any form of politics creates boundaries and barriers, casts molds of the proper form of citizenship and the wrong kinds of people. This is inevitable. Yet such molds exact a price, not only from our ability to be more understanding of others but also from our sense of how we best should live. Sustainable democracy minimizes these risks by bringing such awareness right into democracy's own ontological and epistemological foundations. Paradoxically, in part, it sustains itself by questioning its own borders.

Foundations of some sort, however, must always remain. We have tried to craft a way of looking at environmental and social problems consistent with this notion of democracy. Yet our viewpoint remains subject to the dictates of these standards, even as these standards themselves require interrogation. We now turn to the limits of our own analysis.

Ecology and Individuality

People with democratic temperaments are not usually considered the authors of repressive politics. Certainly liberal environmentalists never see themselves in those terms. Some liberals do see a threat, as André Gorz (1980) suggests, in corporate ecology agendas that would preserve both profits and the environment by further depriving already deprived workers: forcing them to drive and consume less, and to work harder, to make the inescapable environmental transition. Resistance to such an agenda, some fear, might well force closer surveillance of citizens and perhaps even suspension of civil liberties.[1] Such threats are real enough. Corporate environmental agendas are often designed to transform air pollution into toxic trash and then impose that trash on the least powerful communities. Nonetheless, just as corporate solutions to these problems entail costs, risks, and impositions, so too do our own. The process of winning over a constituency for our views—let alone politically implementing them—heightens these dangers, as we hide defects to win support and argue against critics, and do so often under conditions of political contest.

Moreover, the views we present here do not spring pristinely from our minds. They have debts to many of the positions we have critiqued, including free market advocates, social democrats, and even ecofundamentalists. Failing to acknowledge these debts or denying the impositions implicit in our own views could put us on the path to a fundamentalism of our own. We could reflect further on the limits of any of these positions. It is perhaps most appropriate for a work on environmental politics to review the seductions and dangers especially of ecofundamentalism and suggest some ways out.

The seductive promise of ecofundamentalism is its claim to provide new collective and individual identities in a time of social dislocation. Its call to think of ourselves as one big ecofamily is especially appealing as the nuclear family seems less stable. Part of the appeal of the rhetoric of ecofundamentalism is the way metaphors build off and reinforce each other. Michael Shapiro (1989) identifies such a pattern of intertextualization with regard to games and war. If war is seen as a game and Sunday afternoon football games are seen as wars, then it becomes more difficult to give close scrutiny to the nature or significance of each in our lives. If the world is seen as a living being and living beings are seen as functional parts of the world, this rhetorical foray deters us from seeing in either a range of inconsistencies and unpredictabilities. Thus, easy intertextualizations must be resisted—even when the goal is to save the planet.[2]

These concerns must also be addressed for practical reasons. Some people believe that, at its worst, ecofundamentalism implies a kind of friendly fascism. Were this true, it would be the least of our worries. Its rigidity does have consequences, however. The commitment to an all-embracing ideal may force many defenders of present policies to suppress inner doubts and to cling all the more to their own course of action. This commitment may lose support even among citizens concerned about the dangers to nature. Thus, ecofundamentalism can become a breeding ground of support for a kind of corporate fundamentalism—equally rigid and far more likely. For citizens caught in the flux of meanings and identities, the totalizing vision of a community in harmony with nature, in the end, will prove less enticing than the promise of goods, jobs, and income, regardless of environmental effect.

It is not that radical holistic ideals are simply wrong or that connections among work life, family, health, and patterns of growth do not exist—indeed, we argue they do. Rather, such connections and institutions, as human constructions, are a product of past and present needs and expectations and not an unproblematic description of the order of things. The very need to build such connections, and our success in resolving proximate dilemmas by doing so, leads us to view patterns we follow as part of the architecture of things. Because we need such plans, we tend to defend them with a studied blindness to the exclusions they entail.

Democracy, in the words of Reinhold Niebuhr (1960), is best understood as the art of finding proximate solutions to insoluble problems. Our job then goes beyond finding solutions: It is also to loosen the absolute hold of what we find on ourselves and on the polity. In this way, we stand the best chance to enhance the quality of our lives, as well as to allow environmentalism a stronger foothold in our politics. From this perspective, let us look briefly at transit, work, politics, and consumption.

"Joy" Riders, Workaholics, Apathetics, and Shoppers

Transition to a more balanced transit system will not be cost free. No matter how we devise policies, individuals in particular situations—the rural citizen who lives 2 hours from work—will face special difficulties. Gasoline may become more heavily taxed. Carpools may be needed at peak hours near the city. In a society that asks that we depend on the auto less, changes will occur that cannot be expressed monetarily or even in terms of inconvenience. Many people really do need their car. There are also many citizens for whom the speed and independence they feel in their car and its frequent use—even in traffic jams— also become a part of who they are. The pleasure associated with the car is interconnected with other desires and frustrations experienced within the person's life. If environmentalists ever win the day, will this "joy" rider become an object of scorn?

It is not our point here to assess the specifics of transit policy except to suggest that even the most thoughtful and democratically arrived at standards will entail burdens. Policies to foster alternative fuels and transit, therefore, should be crafted with consideration of the damage any regulations—even environmentally sound ones—do. However regulatory problems are resolved, new forms of difference will emerge in response to new standards that themselves are normalizing regimes of their own. Democratic politics informed by an understanding of the burdens entailed even by good policies has the best chance of minimizing the harm of the new orderliness these policies strive to impose.

Surely, a more democratic workplace is valuable because it may reduce extremes of economic inequality while increasing self-esteem and decreasing the need for invidious consumption. It may well be that a workplace that achieves relatively acceptable levels of affluence and opportunities for self-development and leisure time might choose even to retain a certain number of laggards.

If equality is not simply an end in itself but a means toward real individuality, must we expect workplaces to display an identical distribution of rote tasks and creative ones? Should workers who choose to relieve an especially gifted colleague of his or her office chores—perhaps for the good of the enterprise or simply for their own aesthetic appreciation—be discouraged as long as they have opportunities for reasonable self-development.

In addition, the need and the opportunity to develop skills in a workplace setting all too easily translate into all-encompassing norms themselves. What to do with the worker who is satisfied with the relatively static performance of an entry-level job? Should workplaces have policies that mandate certain forms of participation in major company policy areas?

The risk here is that participatory workplaces can create infinitely expandable obligations toward workplace commitment. The very fact that such obligations are constructed through deliberative processes poses its own form of potential coerciveness. It reinforces the need to see in democracy a means not only to make common policies but to protest and limit their excesses.

How important is it that employees avail themselves of the opportunity to reduce hours so that certain forms of community and family life can be strengthened? We argued previously for a right to trade productivity gains for reduced hours at the same pay. But some people "need" to work. How will firms under the new ecological regime treat, and how will society evaluate, individuals who would rather remain workaholics?

Other normalizing implications in the issue of hours reduction can be glimpsed in the work of one of its most impressive early advocates, John Ryan (discussed in Hunnicutt, 1988), a Catholic social theorist of the 1920s and 1930s. Ryan suggested that continuing production of goods and services had become a self-defeating trap for many. He argued that affluence is not an acceptable end for human beings. Rather, it is to be pursued only to the extent that it contributes to broader forms of human fulfillment. Such human fulfillment begins with contributions to family and community and culminates, eventually and most profoundly, in the contemplation of God.

In this regard, the attitude of some American psychologists indebted to Freudian notions of sublimation and the id is revealing. Many worry about time away from work because they see work as providing the discipline needed to move the ego to sublimate a range of instinctual needs (Hunnicutt, 1988). Such sublimation is needed to achieve civilization. The model here is one of the dedicated workplace or civilizing community on the one hand versus anarchic impulses on the other.

Although Ryan's (Hunnicutt, 1988) views are more attuned to the complexities of the self, both views imply that civilization will collapse if some instincts and fantasies are left unchecked. One is tempted to say to Ryan and his modern disciples, but what of frivolous leisure, of time for escape, of art that pokes fun even at those disciplines we know we should follow?

An adequate democratic politics, therefore, is a politics of self as well as of society. By this we do not mean endless interrogation, clarification, and purification. Quite the opposite. Attunement to the dangers of political reforms, which genealogy can suggest, is only a first step. Genealogy, a close examination of our anxieties and their sources and of the partially occluded origins of our values can by itself lead to a quiet despair. But adding cultivation of our own moments of playful and rebellious thoughts, along with respect for those of others, can lead us to celebrate the variety in our world (Connolly, 1993).

Still, many will remain indifferent politically and self-satisfied about who they are. They will unreflectively accept what is simply because it is. They will get on with their lives. Democratic politics can sometimes be demanding and even insistent on participation. But it must always leave room for those who freely choose to withdraw, who resist such speculation, who will not take the trouble to vote. Sustainable democracy does not celebrate passivity but it respects the rights even of apathetics.

However problematic excessive consumption is for the environment and for equity, consumerism remains a realm in which many citizens have carved out a space for some freedom. For the many poor people among us, opportunities for consumption are needed to sustain life or to gain basic entree to the opportunities within our society.

Even for the economically secure, some forms of consumption are not well understood as artificially created needs dictated by advertising or fostered by otherwise alienating lives. Although the experience of shopping can be stressful and invasive, it can also provide a respite from the demands of work and community. Purchasing can become a form of individual, even artful, expression. When trying to limit long hours of work and mitigate a consumerist lifestyle, any democratic politics of ecology must guard against an elitism that would moralistically denigrate such forms of moralistically expression.

No one can guarantee that there is not some degree of conflict between the desire of humans to consume and the ability of the planet to provide adequate resources and disposal capacity. We are confident that much of the talk of inevitable conflict is overblown, a consequence of refusal to examine the relation between consumption and the way we presently orient our politics and economics. Indeed, it is a projection of the zero-sum nature of our social order onto nature, which is then appropriated in defense of that order (Ross, 1994). An orientation to consumerism that (1) makes available some alternatives to the current cycle of working ever harder to shop and spend, (2) emphasizes recyclable or rebuildable forms of consumer goods, and (3) alters the modes by which such goods are produced and shipped promises to reduce such conflicts dramatically. Finally, a political posture that does not demonize consumption or consumers offers the best prospect of winning acceptance for whatever compromises between humans and the planet are necessary.

Conclusions

In the context of these agendas and their limits, we suggest that an adequate sustainability program and discourse involves critique of at least two popular schools of thought on ecology and democracy. A contemporary realist school argues that adequate attention to the demands of the environment will entail major sacrifices that will be unpopular and may well have to be imposed by corporate or government elites (Heilbroner, 1980). Ecopopulist and ecofundamentalist schools argue that a properly organized and managed nogrowth economy will guarantee ecological security and more fulfilling modes of life.

Should we regard nature as a realm of pristine harmony to be worshiped or a reservoir of resources to be hoarded? Part of the wisdom of democracy lies in its ability perpetually to chasten both elite and communal power and thereby open up spaces for nature's surprises. Perhaps the real beauty and appeal of nature, both human and nonhuman, lies in its ability to exceed our theories, and even our dreams, of it.

Those who argue for imposition of sacrifice and those who trumpet completely consensual ecological communities often converge in an apolitical stance. The former ask us to suspend further debate once a policy has been decided. The latter assume that debate can move toward harmonies that perfectly embody our needs and purposes. In our eyes, however, an adequate sustainability discourse must not promise simple solutions of harmonious and natural communities in which politics ends and history is transcended. Nor need it threaten austere ones in which politics must be muted. Fortunately, both invite recalcitrance and resistance. Indeed, so far both have failed to gain acceptance.

Our emphasis on democracy suggests at least two important objections. By continually endorsing the centrality of democratic politics, we seem to have an exhausting vision. Some may even accuse us of a form of political essentialism according to which the true nature of the human person is realized only through political activity.[3] There are, however, already much more powerful pressures against individuality lodged within contemporary society. We see no way to combat these without action by informed and organized citizens.

Market economies and representative polities, which do play a role in nurturing individuality, do not maintain themselves automatically. Indeed, without active political participation in revising and sustaining—and gaining consent for—their values, they can destroy the very conditions of their viability. And willingness to act politically is a crucial defense against political regimes imposing onerous burdens on us. Still, we worry about the degree of political involvement the program we advance asks of people. We do not want to see a world in which excessive hours at work are replaced by endless hours at sometimes mind-numbing meetings. Some of the reforms we call for in Chapters 5 and 6 are designed to make the process of representative government more responsive, more accessible, and less difficult to comprehend. These reforms can then be aided by a skillful blending of representative and some more direct forms of democracy (see Walzer, 1978). But even political participation in a democracy is only one value in lives that already are and always should be constituted in other interesting ways.

Perhaps the best chance to solve our environmental and social problems involves nurturing what's best in our democratic traditions. Through deliberation and discourse we can most effectively evaluate and least onerously design and adminster any answers we find. Through democracy we may come to define our quality of life in ways that impinge far less on the natural world. Indicators of economic progress now need explicitly to include qualitative measures, including the costs incurred to the environment and the real benefits derived by the people, in order to help the public arrive at its own definition of quality. In this work, we have tried to show how a superior quality of life is not only complementary to, but an essential part of, an environmentally sustainable economy. A democratic appeal of a life of higher quality can build support for protecting the environment. It may be democracy alone that is sustainable.

Notes

1. The classic contemporary statement of the possible connection between environmental deterioration and authoritarian politics is Heilbroner (1980).

2. Alexis de Tocqueville speaks of the quiet tyranny of the majority (discussed in Connolly, 1995). In a democratic age, in which every person sees himself or herself as the source of meaning and value, each turns to the masses to buttress his or her own convictions and way of life. Tocqueville sees equality of condition as the cause of this phenomenon and believes it can be combated through small-scale groups, such as voluntary groups or municipal governments, in which individuals have the chance to speak and act and gain a grounded sense of themselves as free and independent individuals. But even Tocqueville's solution runs the risk of claiming finality for the particular group or the process by which it is constituted. In such a context, it becomes appropriate to celebrate democratic politics not simply as a way to frame identities but also as a way to resist the forms of exclusion that even Tocqueville's insights may entail.

3. Donald Moon (1993) discusses the perils of political essentialism. He raises important points, but consistently underplays the dangers to individuality that emanate from concentrations of economic power in present markets.

References

Alperovitz, G., & Faux, J. (1984). *Rebuilding America: A blueprint for the new economy.* New York: Pantheon.

Anderson, J. (1995). Ecosystem ecology and conservation biology: A critique. In T. B. Herman, S. Bondrup-Nielsen, J. H. M. Willison, & N. Munro (Eds.), *Ecosystem monitoring and protected areas* (pp. 45-49). Nova Scotia: Science and Management of Protected Areas.

Arney, W. R., & Bergen, B. J. (1984). *Medicine and the management of living: Taming the last great beast.* Chicago: University of Chicago Press.

Bahro, R. (1985). *Building the green movement.* Philadelphia: New Society.

Barkan, J. (1995, Fall). Symposium on affirmative action. *Dissent,* p. 463.

Bennett, J. (1987). *Unthinking faith and enlightenment: Nature and the state in a post-Hegelian age.* New York: New York University Press.

Bennett, J. (1994). *Thoreau's nature: Ethics, politics, and the wild.* Thousand Oaks, CA: Sage.

Best, M. (1990). *The new competition.* Cambridge, MA: Harvard University Press.

Bluestone, B., & Bluestone, I. (1993). *Negotiating the future.* New York: Basic Books.

Bookchin, M. (1985). Were we wrong? *Telos, 65,* pp. 59-74.

Bookchin, M. (1986). *The modern crisis.* Philadelphia: New Society.

Bowles, S., & Edwards, R. (1993). *Understanding capitalism: Competition, command, and change in the U.S. economy* (2nd ed.). New York: HarperCollins.

Bowles, S., Gordon, D., & Weisskopf, T. (1993). *After the wasteland: A democratic economics for the year 2000.* Armonk, NY: M. E. Sharpe.

Bradley, J. (1994, May/June). On the block: Auctioning off New York City's public works. *Dollars and Sense,* pp. 12-13, 38-40.

Brown, W. (1995). *States of injury: Power and freedom in late modernity.* Princeton, NJ: Princeton University Press.

Buell, J. (1995). *Democracy by other means: The politics of work, leisure, and environment.* Champaign: University of Illinois Press.

Bullard, R. (1993). The anatomy of environmental racism. In R. Hofrichter (Ed.), *Toxic struggles: The theory and practice of environmental justice* (pp. 25-35). Philadelphia: New Society.

Campbell, D. (1992). *Writing security: United States foreign policy and the politics of identity.* Minneapolis: University of Minnesota Press.

Canguilhem, G. (1991). *The normal and the pathological.* New York: Zone.

Clarke, S. A. (1993). Bigger and Booker and the GOP: Race and E/Racing in the struggle for hegemony. In F. M. Dolan & T. L. Dumm (Eds.), *Rhetorical republic: Governing representation in American politics* (pp. 181-198). Amherst: University of Massachusetts Press.

Cocks, J. (1989). *The oppositional imagination.* London: Routledge.

Coles, R. (1992). *Self/power/other: Political theory and dialogical ethics.* Ithaca, NY: Cornell University Press.

Coles, R. (1993). Ecotones and environmental ethics: Adorno and Lopez. In J. Bennett & W. Chaloupka (Eds.), *In the nature of things* (pp. 226-249). Minneapolis: University of Minnesota Press.

Commoner, B. (1990). *Making peace with the planet.* New York: Pantheon.

Connolly, W. (1987). *Politics and ambiguity.* Madison: University of Wisconsin Press.

Connolly, W. (1988). *Political theory and modernity.* London: Basil Blackwell.

Connolly, W. (1992). *Identity/difference: Democratic negotiation of political paradox.* Ithaca, NY: Cornell University Press.

Connolly, W. (1993). *The Augustinian imperative: A reflection on the politics of morality.* Newbury Park, CA: Sage.

Connolly, W. (1995). *The ethos of pluralization.* Minneapolis: University of Minnesota Press.

Daly, H., & Cobb, J. (1989). *For the common good.* Boston: Beacon.

DeLuca, T. (1995). *The two faces of political apathy.* Philadelphia: Temple University Press.

Dickson, D. (1984). *The new politics of science.* New York: Pantheon.

Dockery, D. W., Pope, C. A., Xu, X., Spengler, J. D., Ware, J. H., Fay, M. E., Ferris, B. G., & Spezier, F. E. (1993). An association between air pollution and mortality in six U.S. cities. *New England Journal of Medicine, 329,* 1753-1759.

Dumm, T. L. (1988). The politics of post-modern aesthetics: Habermas vs. Foucault. *Political Theory, 16,* pp. 209-228.

Dumm, T. L. (1994). *United States.* Ithaca, NY: Cornell University Press.

Edsall, T. B., & Edsall, M. D. (1991). *Chain reaction: The impact of race, rights, and taxes on American politics.* New York: Norton.

Ewen, S., & Ewen, E. (1992). *Channels of desire: Mass images and the shaping of American consciousness.* Minneapolis: University of Minnesota Press.

Fairlie, H. (1986). Fear of living. *New Republic, 200*(4), pp. 14-19.

Foster, J. B. (1992). *The limits of environmentalism without class: Lessons from the ancient forest struggle of the Pacific Northwest* (Capitalism/Nature/Socialism Pamphlet Series). Santa Cruz, CA: Capitalism/Nature/Socialism.

French, H. (1990). *Clearing the air: A global agenda* (Worldwatch Paper no. 94). New York: Worldwatch Institute.

Friedman, M. (1962). *Capitalism and freedom.* Chicago: University of Chicago Press.

Garson, B. (1988). *The electronic sweatshop: How computers are transforming the office of the future into the factory of the past.* New York: Simon & Schuster.

Ginsberg, R. (1994). Playing with fire: L.A.'s pollution trading experiment. *Dollars and Sense*(193), pp. 23-25, 42.

Goldman, M. (1993). The tragedy of the commons or the commoners' tragedy? *Capitalism/Nature/Socialism, 3*(4), 49-68.

Goodstein, E. (1995). *Economics and environment.* Englewood Cliffs, NJ: Prentice Hall.

Gordon, L. (1994, Summer). Welfare reform: A history lesson. *Dissent,* pp. 323-328.

Gorz, A. (1980). *Ecology as politics.* Boston: South End.

Gunn C., & Gunn, H. D. (1991). *Reclaiming capital: Democratic initiatives and community development.* Ithaca, NY: Cornell University Press.

Hardin, G. (1977). *Managing the commons.* San Francisco: W. H. Freeman.

Hawken, P. (1993). *The ecology of commerce: A declaration of sustainability.* New York: Harper Business.

Hayden, D. (1984). *Redesigning the American dream: The future of housing, work, and family life.* New York: Norton.

Heilbroner, R. (1980). *An inquiry into the human prospect.* New York: Norton.

Hernstein, R. J., & Murray, C. (1994). *The bell curve: Intelligence and class structure in American life.* New York: Free Press.

Honig, B. (1993). *Political theory and the displacement of politics.* Ithaca, NY: Cornell University Press.

Hunnicutt, B. (1988). *Work without end: Abandoning shorter hours for the right to work.* Philadelphia: Temple University Press.

Illich, I. (1978). *Toward a history of needs.* New York: Random House.

Illich, I. (1981). *Shadow work.* Boston: Marion Boyars.

Kantor, P. (1995). *The dependent city revisited: The political economy of urban development and social policy.* Boulder: Westview.

Kateb, G. (1992). *The inner ocean: Individualism and democratic culture.* Ithaca, NY: Cornell University Press.

Kozol, J. (1991). *Savage inequalities.* New York: Crown.

Kuehls, T. (1996). *Beyond sovereign territory.* Minneapolis: University of Minnesota Press.

Lazonick, W. (1992). Controlling the market for corporate control: The historical significance of managerial capitalism. *Industrial and Corporate Change, 1(1),* 449-486.

Lovins, A., & Lovins, H. (1995). "Reinventing the wheels." *The Atlantic Monthly, 275,* p. 75.

Lynch, R., & Markusen, A. (1994). Can markets govern? *American Prospect, 16,* 125-134.

MacIntyre, A. (1984). *After virtue: A study in moral theory* (2nd ed.). Notre Dame, IN: University of Notre Dame Press.

Mill, J. S. (1965). *Principles of political economy* (J. M. Robson, Ed.). Toronto: University of Toronto Press.

Moon, D. (1993). *Constructing community: Moral pluralism and tragic conflicts.* Princeton, NJ: Princeton University Press.

Morgenson, G., & Eisenstodt, G. (1990, March 5). Profits are for rape and pillage. *Forbes,* pp. 94-100.

Newman, K., & Lennon, C. (1995). The job ghetto. *American Prospect 22,* 67-68.

Niebuhr, R. (1960). *The children of light and the children of darkness.* New York: Scribner.

Niebuhr, R. (1964). *The nature and destiny of man.* New York: Scribner.

New Republic, 213(17). (1994).

O'Connor, M. (1994a). Codependency and indeterminacy: A critique of the theory of production. In M. O'Connor, *Is capitalism sustainable: Political economy and the politics of ecology* (pp. 53-75). New York: Guilford.

O'Connor, M. (1994b). On the misadventures of capitalist nature. In M. O'Connor, *Is capitalism sustainable: Political economy and the politics of ecology* (pp. 125-151). New York: Guilford.

Ophuls, W. (1977). *Ecology and the politics of scarcity.* San Francisco: W. H. Freeman.

Polanyi, K. (1957). *The great transformation: The political and economic origins of our time.* Boston: Beacon.

Quinby, L. (1994). *Anti-apocalypse: Exercises in genealogical criticism.* Minneapolis: University of Minnesota Press.

Rabinow, P. (Ed.). (1984). *The Foucault reader.* New York: Pantheon.

Rifkin, J. (1995). *The end of work: The decline of the global labor force and the dawn of the post-market era.* New York: Jeremy P. Tarcher.

Ross, A. (1994). *The Chicago gangster theory of life: Nature's debt to society.* New York: Verso.

Rousseau, J. (1988). *The social contract* (D. A. Cress, Trans.). Indianapolis: Hackett. (Original published in 1762)

Sale, K. (1985). *Duellers in the land: The bioregional vision.* San Francisco: Sierra Club.

Schor, J. (1991). *The overworked American: The unexpected decline of leisure.* New York: Basic Books.

Schultz, I. (1993). Women and waste. *Capitalism/Nature/Socialism, 4*(2), 51-63.

Scott, H. (1974). *Does socialism liberate women? Experiences from Eastern Europe.* Boston: Beacon.

Shapiro, M. (1989). Representing world politics: The sport/war intertext. In J. Der Derian & M. Shapiro (Eds.), *International/Intertextual Relations.* Lexington: D.C. Health.

Simon, J. L. (1985). Resources, population, environment: An oversupply of false bad news. In G. Berardi (Ed.), *World food, population, and development* (pp. 40-54). Ottawa: Rowman & Allanheld.

Simon, J. A. (1995). More people, greater wealth, more resourses, healthier environment. In J. T. Raulie (Ed.), *Taking sides: Clashing views on controversial issues in world politics* (pp. 297-306). Guilford: Dushkin.

Skocpol, T. (1995). *Social policy in the United States: Future possibilities in historical perspective.* Princeton, NJ: Princeton University Press.

Stevens, W. K. (1995, September 18). Scientists say Earth's warming could set off wide disruptions. *The New York Times,* pp. A1, A8.

Strange, M. (1988). *Family farming: A new economic vision.* Lincoln: University of Nebraska Press.

Strasser, S. (1982). *Never done: A history of American housework.* New York: Pantheon.

Szasz, A. (1994). *Ecopopulism: Toxic waste and the movement for environmental justice.* Minneapolis: University of Minnesota Press.

Taylor, C. (1985a). The concept of a person. In C. Taylor, *Philosophical papers* (Vol. 1, pp. 97-114). Cambridge, UK: Cambridge University Press.

Taylor, C. (1985b). Legitimation crisis? In C. Taylor, *Philosophical papers* (Vol. 2, pp. 248-288). Cambridge, UK: Cambridge University Press.

Thompson, D. (1995, February 27). Congressional chain saw massacre. *Time,* pp. 58-60.

Tyson, L., & Levine, D. (1990). Participation, productivity, and the firm's environment. In A. Blinder (Ed.), *Paying for productivity: A look at the evidence* (pp. 203-204). Washington, DC: Brookings Institution.

Vail, D. (1989). How to tell the forest from the trees: Recent technical changes in the forest industries of Sweden and Maine. In *Technology in society* (Vol. 1, pp. 347-376). Elmford, NY: Pergammon.

Vail, D., Hasund, K. P., & Drake, L. (1994). *The greening of agricultural policy in industrial societies.* Ithaca, NY: Cornell University Press.

Walzer, M. (1978). Town meetings and workers' control: A story for socialists. In M. Walzer, *Radical principles: Reflections of an unreconstructed democrat* (pp. 273-290). New York: Basic Books.

Weil, A. (1990). *Natural health, natural medicine: A comprehensive manual for wellness and self-care.* Boston: Houghton Mifflin.

Wilkins, R. (1995). The case for affirmative action. *The Nation, 260*(12), 409-416.

Winant, H. (1994). *Racial conditions: Politics, theory, comparisons.* Minneapolis: University of Minnesota Press.

Wolff, E. N. (1995). *Top heavy: A study of the increasing inequality of wealth in America.* New York: Twentieth Century Fund.

Worldwatch Institute. (1989). *State of the world, 1989.* New York: Norton.

Yago, G. (1986). *The decline of transit.* Cambridge, UK: Cambridge University Press.

Index

forms of, 130
Reagan Administration, 115
Reagan, Ronald, xiii-xiv, 30, 34
Recycling, viii, 87, 91, 108, 121
    in reference to consumerism, 143
Roosevelt, Franklin, 73, 98, 101, 129
Ross, Andrew, 2, 22
Russell, Bertrand, 66
Ryan,
    views of self, 142
Sandel, Michael, 83-85

Sexism, 128-129
    forms of, 130. *See also* Gender; Women
Shapiro, Micheal, 139
Schor, Juliet, 55
Simon, Julian, 7-13, 48
Skocpol, Theda, 113
Social Security, 113, 129
Stagflation, 30
Subsidies, 109
    auto, 116
    for alternative technologies, 70, 120
    income and tax, 54, 105
Summers, Lawrence, 44
Szasz, Andrew, 43, 49, 57, 133

Taxes, 17, 50-54
    green, 56
    redistribution of, 54
Tax Base, 15, 109
Tax Credits, 117, 118
Tax Policy, 52, 59, 121
Taylor, Charles, 79-81, 84
Taylor, Frederick, 71
Third World:
    as toxic dumps, 44
    exploitation of labor in, 127
Thoreau, 87-89
Three Mile Island, xiv
Toxics, 123, 137
    disposal of, 48, 63-64
    politics of, 46
    risk determined by EPA, 28
    taxing of, 50-54
    waste facilities, 37
Trade, 12, 126-128

free, 104, 108-109
international, 97, 110
policies of, 108
Trade Deficit, 115
Trade Sanctions, 127
Transit Systems, 91
    cost of, 140
    politics of, 128
    policy, 116
    subsidization of, 115

Unemployment, 16, 54, 60-68, 89. *See also* Employment; Jobs
Unions, 73, 108, 124, 125
United Nations, 134
Vail, David, 41

Vietnam, viii, 29, 30

Wages, 111,126
    in Mexico, 127
    in relation to leisure, 141
    low, 16, 108
    stagnation of, 9, 130
Wagner Labor Act, 73
Welfare State, 98, 101
Women, 65-68, 87
    and modern technology, 20
    as mothers, 102-103, 133
    in relation to nature, 129
    in work force, 18, 100, 102, 106
    religious effects on, 20-21, 129. *See also* Gender
Work Hours:
    choice of, 88, 114
    amount of, 17
    reduction of, 141
Workplace, 61, 68-75, 89, 124-126
    and equality, 55, 114
    organization of, 67, 110, 111, 123
    participatory, 141
    policies of, 130

Zoning, 116, 117

About the Authors

John Buell received a BA from Amherst College and an MA in American History from Columbia University and a PhD in political science from the University of Massachusetts at Amherst. He was an associate editor of *The Progressive Magazine* for 10 years and taught political economy at the college level for a number of years. He currently works as a political journalist. His columns and reviews on labor, environment, and the economy have appeared in many local newspapers as well as national political journals such as *The Progressive, In These Times, Commonweal,* and the *Humanist.* He is author of *Democracy by Other Means: The Politics of Work, Leisure, and Environment.*

Tom DeLuca received a BA from Brooklyn College, an MA in political science from the University of Connecticut, and a PhD in political science from the University of Massachusetts at Amherst. He has been a long-time activist on local and national issues, especially nuclear arms control, citizen empowerment, and the environment, and his op-eds have appeared in *The New York Times, The Nation, New York Newsday,* and *The Progressive.* He is currently Assistant Professor of Political Science at Fordham College at Lincoln Center. He recently published The Two Faces of Political Apathy.